THE ROLE OF THE PRESIDENT OF INDIA

Professor Balkrishna

Published by
Frontier India Technology
No 22, 4th Floor, MK Joshi Building, Devi Chowk, Shastri Nagar,
Dombivli West, Maharashtra, India. 421202
http://frontierindia.biz

DEDICATION

This book is dedicated to the common people who make
India a great democracy.

CONTENTS

Acknowledgments   i

1   Foreword   01

2   Preface   03

3   The First President and the Dilemma   06

4   The attrition of Constitutional institution   30

5   President's Role   54

6   About The Author   83

ACKNOWLEDGMENTS

Firstly his wife Smt. Sarla Devi who predeceased him by 20 years and died of cancer but was the pillar of support in his life, Dr. Hem Lata (Gynaec) and Prabha Rao (Architect) his daughters with who he spent most of his time post retirement in Delhi and Mumbai respectively. His sons Devendra, Dharmendra, Hemant and Arun whose support he cherished. Dr. BK Sharma, a dear colleague, Sudharshan who spent many an evening and nights typing the text and all others not mentioned who contributed in his pursuits.

FOREWORD

Shri. Balakrishnaji was a person who was devoted to his motherland, its languages and culture. He participated in the freedom movement. He received lathi blows and was arrested. Throughout his life he wore only Khadi. Yet he would never agree to receive any Tamara Patra or any benefit for his sacrifice. Although entitled, he never used the government trappings like transport etc. even for official use. He was endowed with a brilliant and cool mind. His out of the box line of thinking would sometime annoy other bureaucrat who considered it to be a prestige. I have met few persons who worked so dedicatedly in a government office.

He may rightly be regarded as the father of legal terminology. He was member - Secretary of the Official Language (Legislative) Commission when it was constituted in 1961. In the course of the time the Commission failed to justify its existence. In 1976 when he was the member of Hindi Advisory Committee, he supported the move to wind up the Commission. It was replaced by the Official Language Wing of the Legislative Department.

I had good fortune to see him at work and learn from him. When I was making an effort to get a Constitutional Amendment passed to provide for Authoritative Text of the Constitution in Hindi he gave me full support. Ultimately when the Hindi text was published under the Article 394 A by the Authority of the President in 1986 he was delighted. A dream was fulfilled.

The present book is an example of his original thinking. He argues logically yet takes into account the ground realities of Indian politics. It also shows his deep and abiding concern for evolving a polity that is governed by the law of the Constitution and not by whims, fancies and selfish interests of individuals.

I am sure that the small book will ignite the minds of scholars and drive to amplify and add to what the author has propounded in a small compass.

Brij Kishore Sharma

Brij Kishore Sharma is currently the Chairman of Raja Rammohan Roy Library Foundation, Ministry of Culture, Govt of India. He obtained a LLM degree in 1959 from Lucknow University. He cleared UPSC and joined the Law Ministry in the same year. He worked in various capacities and retired in 1992 as Additional Secretary to the Government of India. He was Chairman, Copyright Board from 2001 - 6. He was also the Chairman of National Book Trust. He authored several books in English and Hindi on law and Legal translation. Introduction to the Constitution of India (7th Edition) and Bharat Ka Sanvidhan : Ek Parichaya (10th edition), are his most popular books.

PREFACE

I was posted in Mumbai in 1993 as the Commander Submarines on the staff of the Commodore Commanding Submarines, (West). The job entailed overseeing the entire gamut of submarine operations on the West coast and one was very busy with little time to oneself. My father Shri. Balkrishna was living with us at Dhanraj Mahal near the Apollo Bunder. He would go for regular walks upto the Radio Club and back. At that time I guess he was writing a book in Hindi on Jurisprudence to be used as a text book for Law students. The Serial Bomb blasts in March '93 in Mumbai and the riots that erupted in their wake affected him a lot. Having been associated with the Freedom struggle, he did not envision such an India that was unfolding then.

Although into his 86th year, he was doing well health wise except for the medication he used to take for his heart condition. He led a very austere life, a teetotaler. His sole treasure in life was his books and single minded pursuit of knowledge. The riots and the aftermath sapped his will to live on. He stopped taking his medicines and in end April suffered a massive heart attack on 28th of April and never really recovered from it and breathed his last in the early hours of 01 May 1993.

After completing his last rites, I travelled on leave to Delhi to visit my elder sister, at whose house in Kashmere Gate, My father used to spend his time in Delhi and where most of his papers were kept. Whilst in Delhi amid sorting out his papers, I recall contacting Dr. Lokesh Chandra, son of Dr. Rhagu Vira, presently the President, Indian Council of Cultural Research (ICCR) and a scholar in his own right, to inform him of my father's passing away. My father was a friend of Dr. Raghu Vira as both were scholars and linguists. Dr. Chandra urged me to sift my father's papers and get some of his works published as he felt that such an act would be the best tribute to my Father's memory.

The nurse who was on duty in INHS Asvini, the Naval Hospital where my father had been in the ICCU prior to breathing his last, told me that just before he had gone, he had wondered to her as to who would complete the book he was writing at that time. The book was indeed completed in 2009, courtesy Dr. B.K. Sharma, who had been with my father in the Official Languages (Leg) Commission. The same was published and was awarded a prize by the Government of India, a couple of years ago.

My sister did mention to me that our father had written a treatise on the 'Role of The President of India' and that it should be in his papers. She knew of it because her lawyer husband's PA, Sudharshan used to type the script. I remembered that he used to talk about it with us. My wife Deepa had preserved the typescript through our moves on various transfers. It took some time before I was able to ferret out the typescript but was not able to follow up on it for some time due to my pre occupation with my work. When I did get an opportunity to explore its publication, I was rather disappointed as a few of those I approached wanted it to be spruced up and made a bit sensational. I was not prepared to alter the text in any manner as that would have amounted to dishonouring my father's work. He would have wanted it presented as it was. The matter lay there for some years, till recently, Frontier India showed interest in publishing as it is.

As regards the subject matter of the book itself is concerned, the main issue is relevant today as it could ever be. The law in respect of appointment of the Judges to the courts has been changed twice, first in 1993 introducing the Collegium system and recently by the National Judicial Appointment Commission Act. To that extent the template may have changed but the main theme of the treatise on the Role of the President retains its focus.

Shri. Balkrishna, my father, was a scholar and a great intellect. In my personal life, I have rarely seen a man so widely read and knowledgeable on various subjects we encounter in our lives. Be it philosophy, religion, history, law even basic sciences, his knowledge was extremely vast. He was also a linguist and knew many Indian Languages Sanskrit, Hindi, Bengali, Gujarati. He also knew French and German. I was always fascinated by the vast library of books that he had. I donated the bulk of them numbering nearly a thousand to the Bhandarkar Oriental Research Institute in Pune a few years back.

It is sincerely hoped that the book will elicit interest in the Legal and constitutional fraternity.

Commodore Arun Kumar, AVSM,NM. (Retd.)
Pune.
May 2015.

THE FIRST PRESIDENT AND THE DILEMMA

The question as to what role the President of India had to play in the governance of India under the Constitution came to be raised soon after the Constitution came into force on the 26th January 1950. Dr. Rajendra Prasad had been elected by the Constituent Assembly of India to be the interim President with effect from the date the Constitution of India came into force that is to say with effect from 26th January 1950. On that day he took the oath before assuming the office of the interim President, he undertook thereby to preserve, protect and defend the Constitution and the law to the best of his ability. Being a person, who was God fearing and who naturally felt bound to remain true to his oath, he felt it absolutely essential to have a clear perception of what he was expected to do in pursuance of the provisions of the Constitution so that he may not even inadvertently transgress any of those provisions. He, therefore, drew up an exhaustive list of the provisions of the Constitution whereby the President was required to take any kind of action. He sent that list to the Prime Minister of India, namely, Pt. Jawaharlal Nehru with a query as to what exactly was the President expected to do in accordance with these provisions. As the President was not satisfied with what the Prime Minister's reply in the matter was, so it was ultimately referred to Shri. M.C. Setalvad, the then Attorney General, for his opinion.

Shri Setalvad opined that the President was required to

act in the exercise of his functions on the advice of the Council of Ministers as laid down in Article 74 of the Constitution. At that time the relevant clause of the said Article was as follows:

"74. Council of Minister to aid and advise President: (1) There shall be a Council of Ministers with the Prime Minister at the head to aid and advise the President in the exercise of his functions."

But as it could be urged that while the President was to take the advice of the Council of Ministers before acting in the exercise of his functions, he was not necessarily bound to abide by that advice, so Shri. Setalvad averred that the term *'advice'* had come to mean binding advice in Constitutional practice.

Thus in his view the President had no independent role to play in the Government. of India. It may be mentioned that by that time there had been no occasion for the Supreme Court to express their opinion in respect of this question in any disputed matter that had come up to them for adjudication. The Attorney General appeared to have been influenced in his, above mentioned, opinion by what happens in Great Britain in so far as the nominal head, namely, the King, is concerned. As the Constitution of India provided for the establishment of a system of Cabinet government, so it could be plausibly argued that the role of the President of India was similar to that of the King of England which was to give advice to the Prime Minister and the Cabinet ministers, which the latter were naturally to respect but were not bound to follow. The Supreme Court has also agreed in a case (AIR 1955 SC 549) that we have the same type of executive as in the United Kingdom. The Indian Presidency thus became merely a costly symbol of national unity without having any powers of its own to act in its discretion even in crucial matters as the application of Articles 352 and 356 of the Constitution. Dr. Prasad, however, did not feel fully satisfied as to the correctness of the opinion of the

Attorney General. It must be remembered that Dr. Rajendra Prasad had himself been a distinguished lawyer as also the President of the Constituent Assembly. He therefore felt that the matter needed further examination.

So when I joined the personal staff of the President as his Press Attaché, he felt that in view of my earlier experience as a teacher of Constitution to graduate and postgraduate classes, he could entrust me that work of the further examination of the issue on a confidential basis. It is well known that Dr. Rajendra Prasad was a person of extremely modest nature and was very averse to raising any public controversies in so far as his own personal position or interests were concerned. In this case also he did not want to become the centre of any personal controversy notwithstanding his apprehension that unless the ambiguity in the Constitutional role of the president in the governance was removed, he may inadvertently act in violation of his oath 'to preserve, protect and defend the Constitution and the law'. In any case he asked me to make an exhaustive study of the matter and submit a note of the result of my study to him. As directed, I made a fresh examination of the Constitutions of Great Britain, Canada, Australia, United States *vis-à-vis* the Constitution of India, and on the basis of that study drew up a note for the consideration of the President.

In the course of the study it became clear to me that the basic premise on which the opinion in respect of the position of the President of India had been made by the law authorities of the Government of India and by other Constitutional Pandits, namely, that India like Great Britain had a Cabinet system of government and consequently the head of state in India necessarily had the same Constitutional position as the King or Queen of Great Britain had, was not wholly correct for at least two reasons.

In the first place, some element of similarity did not mean complete identity between the governmental systems of the two countries. There were vital differences as well between their governmental systems. Under the Constitution of Great Britain, the system of government is completely unitary in character whereas the government system in India under the Constitution of India (as that Constitution had come into force on the 26th January 1950) was neither wholly federal nor wholly unitary but was of a unique category of its own and in a way unparalleled in the whole world. In the second place the milieu in which the government had to function in India was totally different from what existed in Great Britain. It is now a well-established and generally recognised fact that the actual functioning of a government, even though quite identical in form to the government of another country, having a different social milieu, is conditioned by the social milieu of the country and consequently differs considerably from the functioning of the government of the other.

Inevitably, therefore, the governmental system of the two, namely, India and Great Britain were bound to function differently to a considerable extent.

Consequently, it was wholly improper to make an assessment of the role of the President of India on the basis of an analogy between the President of India and the King or Queen of Great Britain as heads of State. On the contrary, the role of the President of India in the Governance of India must be ascertained by an intrinsic examination of the constitution of India itself and the social milieu within which that constitution has necessarily to operate. This examination must be made without any preconception about how similar political institutions have been found to function in other democratic countries of the world.

In undertaking that intrinsic examination it did not appear proper to give any determinative significance to what was said in the Constituent Assembly about the Presidential office when it was under consideration therein. One of the principles of statutory interpretation which has been repeatedly laid down by the highest courts in the countries including India where the common law jurisprudence prevails is that the provisions of the enactments should be interpreted as they are in accordance with the rules of grammar of the language in which they have been drawn up and not in accordance with the opinions expressed about them when those were under discussion in the relevant legislature. It is true that sometime after 1950, and even recently it had been ruled by the Supreme Court of India, that in the case of ambiguity of language making it extremely difficult to extract the import of the provisions under question, a reference may be made to the debate in the Legislature in respect thereof (AIR 1998 SC 2239 UP Bhoodan Yagna Samiti, UP v Braj Kishore paras 11, 12, 13, 14, 15 and others). But there appeared to be no ambiguity in the provisions of the Constitution relating to the office of the President and so it was not necessary to refer to the debates of the Constituent Assembly for gathering their import.

The first distinctive and notable provision of the Constitution that attracted attention was the one relating to the election of the President. It was sui generis, and is set out in Article 54 of the constitution. It is provided therein that "The President shall be elected by the members of an electoral college consisting of:

The elected members of both Houses of Parliament, and

The elected members of the Legislative Assemblies of the States.

But as the States are of varying sizes and they differ very widely in the strength of their population, the fathers of the constitution felt that a provision must be made to secure uniformity in the scale of representation of the different States at the election of the President and accordingly, they enacted Article 55 to secure that uniformity. They also set out in Clause (2) of that Article the method whereby that uniformity was to be secured. They also provided that there shall be parity of voting strength between the States as a whole on the one hand and the Union on the other and for the realization of that objective they set out the method of securing that parity also in that Article.

1,Queen Victoria Road,
New Delhi.
3-7-48.

I have known Shri Balkrishna ever since I had been visiting Pilani(Rajputana) while he was a professor there in Birla College. He had occasions to come in close contact with me. It is with great pleasure that I testify that I have found him a person of exceptional intelligence,wide scholarship,industrious habits and moral integrity. He has acquitted himself creditably in the discharge of his duties. I strongly recommend him for appointment in the Indian Administrative Service or any other Service of the same status.

(Rajendra Prasad)

This provision in respect of the election of the President is evidently intended to ensure that the Constituent States shall have a role in the election of the President equal to that of the Union. In other words, the President elect shall not be a mere nominee of the Union but shall equally be a nominee of the Constituent States as well. Thus the Constituent States shall have in the President a guardian and upholder of their interests just as the Union shall have in the President a custodian of its interests as well. By this method of election the President becomes, so to say, the one person who represents all the Constituent States as also the Union at the same time and is consequently expected to look after the interests of both the Union and the Constituent States with impartiality and equal zeal. He has consequently to remain on a pedestal, which is above that of both the Union and the Constituent States. His position is thus unique amongst the heads of democratic as also Republican States. In a way he has to maintain a balance between the interests of the Union on the one hand and those of the Constituent State on the other. Thus his position is wholly different from that of the King or Queen of Great Britain. The latter comes to occupy the office of the monarchy in accordance with the principle of heredity. But the continued operation of this principle depends for all practical purposes on the sweet will of the two Houses of Parliament in general and the House of Commons in particular. So the position of the King or Queen become considerably weakened vis-à-vis the House of Commons and the Cabinet, which controls that House. Thus, the equation between the King or Queen on the one hand and the elected representations of the people of Great Britain, namely, the House of Commons and the Cabinet on the other hand. This equation has been fixed by historical forces and has remained so fixed for quite a long time. But in the case of the President there had been no earlier historical forces to fix that equation and it has yet to be determined.

Another notable point was that Prime Minister of the Union could not but be a partisan politician as he had to be the nominee of a political party, which at the relevant time had secured a majority of seats in the Lok Sabha at a

General Election held for that Sabha. But the members of that Sabha and the elected leader of that House could normally, politically and legally claim to have been chosen by the adult population of India only to handle those matters alone which have been allotted to the Union by the Constitution. They could not lay claim to be chosen to deal with the affairs which have been exclusively allotted to the Constituent States by the Constitution. The Union Government has, no doubt, been authorized by the Constitution to issue directions in respect of certain matters to the Constituent States. Under articles 256, 257 [(1), (2) and (3)], these matters are :

(a) The obligation of the Constituent States to exercise their executive power so as to ensure its compliance with the laws made by the Parliament and any existing laws which apply in the concerned States. (Article 256)

(b) Obligation of the Constituent States to exercise their executive power so as not to impede or prejudice the exercise of the executive powers of the Union. (Article 257 (1))

(c) The construction and maintenance of means of communication declared by the Rajya Sabha to be of national or military importance. (Article 257 (2))

(d) Protection of Railways within every one of the Constituent States. (Article 257 (3))

But the scope of the power of issuing directions to the Constituent States for the above purposes is quite limited in as much as the power of the Union Parliament to make laws is limited by the provisions of Articles contained in Chapter I of part 21 of the Constitution. Obviously, this limited power of issuing directions to the Constituent States does not and cannot make the Union council of

Ministers and its leader namely the Union Prime Minister and the members of the majority party in the two Houses of Parliament the custodian of the entire life of India in the sense and to the extent in or to which the President of India, as the Elect of the Nation, is by virtue of his oath of office the ultimate guardian of the entire life of the Indian people.

It was thus evident that the position of the Prime Minister of the Union of India was Constitutionally quite different from that of the Prime Minister of Great Britain in as much as in Great Britain there is not and cannot be any authority other than the Cabinet which under the constitution of Great Britain has a distinct position, influence and power of its own in any specified area of Great Britain and which has or can have any comparison with that of the Prime Minister of that country whereas in India the chief Ministers of States do have Constitutionally an independent source of their own power within the state. However, in one respect there is some measure of similarity between the Prime Minister of Great Britain and that of the Union of India in as much as both of them do have the Constitutional privilege of getting the lower House of the respective Parliaments dissolved before their prescribed term of five years. By virtue of this privilege they can keep a kind of sword of Damocles hanging over the members of those Houses and can keep those members within their control to a great extent. In Great Britain, the Prime Minister has thus acquired the character of a plebiscitary dictator over the entire functioning of the British Polity. But in the case of India the Union Prime Minister is not in a position Constitutionally to become a plebiscitary dictator by virtue of his above mentioned privilege because of the special and unique features of the Indian polity which are quite visible and are set out hereinafter.

This difference between the positions of the Prime Minister of Great Britain on the one hand and the Prime

Minister of the Indian Union on the other made the nature of power equation between the British Crown with the Prime Minister of his country quite different from the power equation that was Constitutionally provided from between the President of India on the one hand and the Union Prime Minister on the other.

Another material difference between the position of the King or Queen of Great Britain and that of the President of India was seen to be in respect of their respective tenure of office. While in Great Britain the King or Queen remains on his or her throne only so long he or she maintains a harmonious relationship with the Cabinet and the House of commons notwithstanding their ascending the throne on the basis of the hereditary principle. The President of India remains in his office for five years even though he may not be fully in harmony with the Union Council of Ministers and the Union Prime Minister and even with the majority of the members of the Lok Sabha. Edward VIII had to abdicate his throne simply because his proposed marriage to Wally Simpson was not being approved by his ministers. It was thus obvious that once the King or Queen falls out with the Cabinet, he or she has no option but to leave his or her headship of the state. But in the case of the President of India the position in this respect appeared to be quite different. If the President of India fell out with his Council of Ministers, he could still hope to come back to his office notwithstanding his resigning initially on his acute difference with the Union Council of Ministers commanding a majority in the Lok Sabha. This possibility is there because of the provision of Article 57 and 62 of the Constitution. In 1950 it was not obvious that a situation could arise in which the party or parties in power in the Constituent States could be wholly opposed to the party in power at the Union level because at that time the Congress Party had such a dominating position in popular esteem that it was obvious that it would easily win at the General Election to the Lok

Sabha as also at the General Election to the Assemblies of the Constituent States. But it appeared to me even then that this situation in respect of the Congress party could well change in the foreseeable future. It may well happen that the Congress party may win majority in the Lok Sabha and later on the election to the Assemblies of the Constituent States, parties opposed to the Congress may win overwhelmingly either on account of a sea change in public opinion all over the country or on account of local considerations and pulls. It was also obvious that there was no inevitability that General Elections be held simultaneously for the Lok Sabha and the Legislative Assemblies of all the States. On account of the provisions of Article 173 and 175 of the Constitution, the Legislative Assembly of a State could be dissolved before the expiry of its term of five years. As dissolutions of the Assemblies of different States may take place at different times so General Elections to them were bound to be held at different times. It could, therefore, be anticipated that in future it may well happen that in the State Legislative Assemblies there may be parties in power which were firmly opposed to the party in power at the Union level. In that event the complexion of the Electoral College empowered to elect the President may be such as to favour a candidate who was set up by the parties opposed to the party in power at the union level. In such a situation the President who refuses to act according to the advice of the Union Council of Ministers or of the Union Prime Minister and thereupon resigns his office but offers himself for re-election to the office of the President would have every chance of getting the support of the parties in power in the Constituent States and would thus be able to get elected to the office of the President even in the face of the opposition of the Union Prime Minister's supporters in the electoral College.

In this respect the position of the President is quite different also from that of the President of the United

States. In the case of the latter, the Vice-President succeeds to the office of the President for the remaining term of the President in the event of the latter's resignation or permanent incapacity to discharge the duties of his office. Thus the President of India, who must be a well-known political leader to be elected to that office, is in a much better position to stand his ground against the Prime Minister of the Union than is the King or Queen of Great Britain. The latter leases his or her office for the rest of his or her life on account of being compelled to abdicate the throne on his or her failing to abide by the advice of the Prime Minister of Great Britain, whereas the President of India would lose at worst his office for a term of few years even if he cannot hope to be re-elected but if the circumstances are what have been stated above, he would not incur any risk of losing his office except for the short time that elapses between his resignation and his re-election. In case he is re-elected in the circumstances set out   above, it will be for the Prime Minster to resign his office.

Still another notable and in a sense determining difference between the Indian Constitution on the one side and the Constitutions of England, France and even that of the United States of America on the other, lay in the provisions relating to the proclamation of emergency and the assumption by the President, of the government of the Constituent State wherein a situation had arisen in which the governance could not be carried on in accordance with the provisions of the Constitution. A drastic provision like that of Article 356 is not to be found in the Constitutions of those States, which have a federal form of government, e.g. Australia and Canada. In the United States of America the Federal Government cannot on its own initiative, intervene in the affairs of a state even if there is an insurrectionary situation in that state. Only if the Governor of the concerned state invites federal intervention in such a situation, the President as the head of the federal executive can intervene. There is no parallel provision in the Constitutions of Canada and Australia, which have Federal Constitutions. This unique provision in the Indian Constitution casts a duty on the President to exercise the power granted to him by that Article namely Article 356 so as not to give an impression that he was guided by the objective of promoting the interests of the party in power at the Union level and of the Prime Minister of the Union Government as against the interests of the ruling party of the concerned state. In 1950, it was not easy to visualise, herein before stated above, that the Government of a Constituent State would be in the hands of a party which was opposed to the Congress Party which was ruling at the Union level. Naturally, it did not appear that the power granted by Article 356 was capable of being misused by the ruling political party or its leader ruling at the Union level. But in my above mentioned note, I said that this possibility may arise if the view that the President was bound to abide by the advice of the Union Council of Ministers and in actual practice by the advice of the Prime Minister of the Union at all times and in all circumstances, were held to be correct. It could be visualized that a party opposed to the Congress Party may capture power at an election held at a time when general election to the Lok Sabha was not being held nor was due to be held. As stated herein before, there was absolutely no reason to hold the view that there always, would or could be simultaneous General elections for both the Lok Sabha and the Assemblies of all the Constituent States. There was bound to be a General Election for the Legislative Assembly of a Constituent State at a wholly different time from that of the General Election to the Lok Sabha. Naturally, as explained herein before there was every possibility of a political party radically opposed to the ruling party at the Union level to come into power in the States.

It was also probable that a confrontation may occur between the Government of a State and the Union

Government and the Prime Minister of the Union may desire that the Government of that State be dislodged from the seat of power and may advise the President to have recourse to the provisions of Article 356 to dismiss that state government and impose President's rule in that state. The question I raised was whether the President was bound to abide by such an advice of the Prime Minister of the Union even if there had not been a Constitutional deadlock or breakdown in that state. Article 356 speaks of the satisfaction of the President on the report of the Governor of the state or otherwise that "a situation has arisen in which the Governance of the State cannot be carried on in accordance (Article 257 (1)) with the provisions of the Constitution". In view of his duty to act in a non-partisan spirit in accordance with his oath of office, this satisfaction of the President has to be his own, and not that of the Prime Minister of the Union. Consequently, if the Prime Minister of the Union advises the President to take over the administration of concerned State because in the former's opinion there has been a breakdown of the Constitutional processes in that state, then the President was not necessarily bound to act in accordance with that advice but had to satisfy himself that the said advice of the Prime Minister was not out of malice towards the Party in power in that state but was based on facts which conclusively revealed that situation had indeed arisen in which it was not possible that the governance of the State could be carried on in accordance with the provisions of the Constitution. I asserted this because President of India was Constitutionally above party politics and was thus in a position to take a dispassionate and non-partisan view of the situation while the Union Council of Ministers and its leader namely the Prime Minister were wedded to party interests and could not be expected necessarily to take a non-partisan view of the situation on the basis of which an opinion could be formed as to the impossibility of the governance of the

State being carried on in accordance with the provisions of the Constitution. I felt that this provision made it clear that the President was not a mask under the cover of which the Government of the Union and its Council of Ministers carried on the business of the Indian Polity as a whole.

My examination of the Constitution of Canada and Australia also led me to the view that the advice of the Union Council of Ministers was not necessarily binding in character. The Act of Parliament, which laid down the Constitution of Canada, had used the expression 'Governor General in Council' where the Governor General was to act in accordance with the advice of the Council of Ministers and the expression 'Governor General' where the Governor General could act on his own. This was also the case in so far as the Parliament's Act laying down the Constitution of Australia was concerned. Both these Constitutions are federal in character. On their basis therefore, it could be said that in a Federal Government, the use of the expression of advice in a Constitutional document did not necessarily imply that it was binding in character.

Moreover, the fact that, the President was to act on the advice of the Election Commission in the matter of the incurrence of disqualification by a person elected to either house of the Union Parliament or to any those of the Legislature of a state made it clear that there were matters on which the Council of Ministers or the Prime Minister of the Union had no role to play and had no right whatever to advise the President. Thus it could not be said that the term "President' used in any Article of the Constitution implied only the Council of Ministers and not the individual person holding for the time being the office of the President.

One argument that had been put forward by those asserting that the President was bound by the advice of the Council of Ministers just as the King or Queen of Great Britain is so bound was that even in Great Britain the King or Queen was legally vested with powers which are plenary in character but as pointed out by Walter Bagehot, conventions have arisen which have made the King or Queen act in accordance with whatever advice was given to him or her by the Cabinet. Indeed, it has been asserted by some authors writing about the Constitution of Great Britain that the King or Queen of Great Britain has no option but to give assent to a Bill of Attainder whereby he or she were being given capital punishment. But this argument appeared to be fallacious because no conventions could be said to have developed in 1950 in respect of the office of the President as that office and the Constitution which created it had come into existence only on the 26th January 1950. It could be said that the Constitutional conventions had evolved in Great Britain under the pressure of the political circumstances existing from time to time in history of Great Britain. These were not inherent features of the system of Cabinet government. There was Cabinet government in the third French Republic. But the sort or conventions, which existed in Great Britain in the sphere of Constitutional practice, were not all to be found in the working of the Cabinet government in France. It could not be said, therefore, that the Constitutional conventions of Great Britain ipso facto attached to the Constitution of India simply because it made provision for the Cabinet system of government. Indeed, the Constitution of India had incorporated only one Constitutional convention of Great Britain. It was in respect of the immunities and privileges of the members of the two Houses of Parliament of the Union and of the Legislatures of the Constituent States. There being no mention of other Constitutional conventions of Great Britain in the Indian Constitution as it stood in 1950 so it could not be said that all the Constitutional conventions of Great Britain had come to be attached to the working of the Constitution of India.

This point had special significance in so far as the

union legislature was concerned. In Article 111 it is laid down that a Bill after having been passed by both the Houses of Parliament shall be presented to the President and the President shall declare either that he assents to the Bill or that he withholds assent therefrom. Now this article was enacted by the constituent Assembly at a time when it was well known that the King or Queen or Great Britain could not withhold his or her assent to any legislative measure passed by the two Houses of the Parliament of Great Britain. If the Constituent Assembly had no intention to empower the President to veto any Bill passed by the two Houses of Union Parliament then it need not have inserted the expression 'withhold his assent' in Article 111 of the Constitution. If that August body wanted to give the President a limited power of vetoing any such Bill, they could have made a provision for overriding the veto of the President such as the one which obtains in the Constitution of the United States of America. But no such provision was made by that August body. So it could be naturally held that the President had the unqualified power to veto any Bill passed by the two Houses of the Parliament.

Another point that struck me was that if the President was required always to act in accordance with the advice tendered to him by the Council of Ministers, then there was no reason whatever to make any Constitutional provision for his impeachment for violation of the Constitution. But the constituent Assembly had made such a provision in Article 61 of the Constitution. In the Constitution of the United States the provision for the impeachment of the President had to be made because the President there had been given powers, which were quite extensive in character and could be personally misused by him.

The provisions of Article 61 are somewhat parallel to the provision in the Constitution of the United States of America in respect of the impeachment of the President.

Such a provision in the Constitution of India in the year 1950 could have any utility or justification only if it was anticipated that the President of India would have an effective opportunity to misuse the powers granted to him.

```
                                        New Delhi.
                                The 27th February, 1948.

        To whom it may concern.


                I happen to come in close contact with
        Prof. Balkrishna as he is assisting us in the Hindi
        translation of the Constitution of India. I understand
        his educational career has been very brilliant and
        he was in a responsible position as Prof. & Head of
        the History Department in Birla College, Pilani,
        which permanent post he left to be of service of the
        Constituent Assembly of India.

                I hold very high opinion about him. He is
        highly intelligent and painstaking and has knowledge
        of legal and constitutional subtlities not usually
        found in a young man of his  age and has an analytical
        mind well fitted to the work requiring research on
        such subjects.

                                        (G. S. Gupta).
```

But if the idea of the fathers of the Constitution was that the President would have always to act in accordance with the advice given to him by the Council of Ministers then no occasion could arise when there could be a misuse of any provisions of the Constitution by the President, and so there could be no reason whatever to make a specific provision for his impeachment in the Constitution. Indeed, even the specific provision for his swearing or solemnly affirming that he shall preserve, protect and defend the Constitution and the law would have been meaningless if the President was not to have any power to fulfill the duty cast on him by that oath or solemn affirmation. These two provisions in the Constitution necessarily implied that the President of India shall have some power which he could personally use to fulfill the duty cast on him by his oath or solemn affirmation and which power could be misused by him.

The points mentioned above were elaborated in the note I was then preparing for submission to the President in 1950 about forty years ago. But I do not remember whether I also referred in that note to the significance of Articles 75 and 78 of the Constitution. I have however reason to presume that I could not have missed the significance of the said articles in relation to the power that the President could exercise on his own and in respect of the exercise of which there could not be any question of the advice of the Union Council of Ministers, and must have referred to the import of those articles.

Article 75(I) provides that the "Prime Minister shall be appointed by the President". Evidently, there can be no question of any advice being given to the President by the Council of Ministers in respect of such appointment. Ivor Jennings does say that in Great Britain the outgoing Prime Minister suggests to the King or Queen as to whom should he or she call for forming the Ministry after the party, which was in power prior to the General Election to the House of Commons has been defeated at the Election. But even there, this advice is only of a formal nature because the person who is the leader of the party that has won is already known and advice or no advice, the King or Queen is already aware of the person who is to be entrusted with the commission of forming the Ministry. In India, no such convention existed in 1950 as prior to that date there had not developed any two party system, nor by that date there had been any possibility of any party other than the Congress Party having a majority in the Houses of Union Parliament. So this power of appointment of the Prime Minister of the Union had to be exercised by the President keeping in view the party position existing after a General Election to the Lok Sabha, but in his own individual judgment and not on the advice of the outgoing Council of Ministers. There is another implication to this power of the President. The power of appointment normally contains within itself the power of dismissal. In the case of the permanent executive specific provision is made in the Constitution itself if it is intended that the members of the permanent executive must be shielded from being victimized by the political Executive for reasons wholly extraneous to the rules of conduct applicable to them. In the case of the political Executive, no such provision is necessarily to be made because their tenure depends on their political fortunes. It is this fact that is given recognition in Article 75 itself when provision is made therein that Ministers shall hold their office during the pleasure of the President. The Prime Minister also being a Minister holds office during the pleasure of the President. Thus the President does have the power of dismissing the Prime Minister whenever he withdraws his pleasure from him. Of course, this withdrawal can occur only if it becomes evident to the President that notwithstanding the Prime Minister having a majority in the Lok Sabha to which he is Constitutionally responsible, he and his party have become extremely unpopular and have lost the confidence and support of a vast majority of the electorate, and so can be dismissed without there being any risk of the action of the President evoking a bitter and severe popular reaction. The President can overcome the hostile reaction of the majority in the Lok Sabha to the dismissal of the Prime Minister by dissolving the Lok Sabha in exercise of the power granted to him by Article 85(2)(b) of the Constitution. It is, however, evident that such a drastic step as the dismissal of the Prime Minister commanding a majority in the Lok Sabha carries with it a great political risk to the President and would be taken only in extraordinary circumstances by a President who commands great political support in the whole country and is convinced that such a step has to be taken to fulfil the duty cast on him by his oath or solemn affirmation to "preserve, protect and defend the Constitution and the Law". Morally such a step would not appear to the electorate to be proper and defensible if taken by the President for personal aggrandizement or out of personal malice against the Prime Minister. In other words the power granted to him by Article 75 is a reserve power to be exercised only when the President has no option left in so far as the maintenance of the Constitution and the law is concerned. It is a radical remedy for a deadly political disease such as the corruption of the Ministry and the party supporting it or treasonable acts on the part of the Prime Minister. Ordinarily, the President has to keep himself aloof from the arena of peaceful political contest between different political parties. But with all the reservations about the use of power of the dismissal of the Prime Minister it can be said that in respect of the exercise of this power there can be no question of the President acting on the advice of the Council of Ministers for no Prime Minister or the Council of Ministers would ask for his or their own dismissal. Apart from dismissal there can be situations in which the President may be requested to take some other action, which is adverse or prejudicial to the Prime Minister. In such a situation also the President shall have to take a decision in the exercise of his best judgment and not on the advice of the Council of Ministers. Thus it is evident that in so far as the area of appointment and dismissal of the Prime Minister or any other legally obligatory action, which is prejudicial to the Prime Minister is concerned, it is outside the area in which the advice of the Council of Ministers has necessarily to be taken.

The implications of Article 78 are of a similar character. There can be no question of the advice of the Council of Ministers in respect of the obligation cast on the Prime Minister to do what the President may require him to do under clauses (2) and (3) of that Article and of the Prime Minister's duty to furnish to the President such "information relating to the administration of the affairs of the union and the proposals for legislation as the President may call for". The Constitution does not make the provisions of Article 78 subject to the provisions of Article 74 nor to any other Article. Thus there can be no situation in which the Prime Minister could evade or avoid the fulfillment of the duty cast on him by Article 78 nor can the Council of Ministers absolve the Prime Minister from the fulfillment of the duty cast on him by that Article.

In respect of the appointment of the judges of the Supreme Court, the Constitution provides that the President shall make such appointments "after consultation with such of the judges of the Supreme Court and of the High Courts in the States as the President may deem necessary for the purpose" and that in the case of the judges other than the Chief Justice of the Supreme Court, the President shall always consult the Chief Justice of the Supreme Court of India. In the case of the appointment of the puisne Judges of the High Courts, the President is required to consult the Chief Justice of India, the Chief Justice of the concerned High Court and the Governor of the concerned State. In the case of the Chief Justice of a High Court, the President is to make his appointment after consulting the Chief Justice of India and the Governor of the concerned State. The Constitution does not specifically provide that in making such appointments the President would be bound by the advice of the Union Council of Ministers or of the Prime Minister of the Union or the Chief Minister of the concerned state. Considering that the Constitution provides for an independent judiciary, it appeared that the main consideration to be kept in view was to be the legal acumen and the moral standing of the person in the matter of his or her selection for appointment as a Judge of the Supreme Court or of any High Court. Political connections and convictions were not to be given any weight. It was inevitable that the Council of Ministers at the Union level or at the State level would be of some political party and would be susceptible to political considerations in giving their advice in respect of appointments of such judges. The Constitution has made specific provision in Article 233 and 234 to ensure that even district judges and other judges of the inferior courts are selected and appointed independently of the political executive of the Constituent States. It could, therefore, be presumed that in the selection of the judges for the Supreme Courts as well, the same consideration was required to prevail by the Constitution. Thus even if the Council of Ministers gave its advice in respect of the selection and appointment of any person as the judge of the Supreme Court or of any High Court, the President was not bound to abide by that advice and was to give greater weight to the advice of the Chief Justice of India.

Thus on this intrinsic examination of the Constitution my conclusion was that the President of India is not like the President of France under the Constitution of the Third Republic whose sole virtue was impotency. He did have powers, which he could exercise on his own and also powers which were exercised after receiving the advice of the Council of Ministers. Even in respect of the second category of powers he was not necessarily bound to act in accordance with the advice of the Council of Ministers but could disregard that advice in some special situations. Normally, he would act in accordance with that advice simply because the Government of the Union had to be carried on and that also according to democratic norms. It was expected that neither the President nor the Prime Minister and the Council of Ministers should carry their differences to the bitter end but should, in the interests of the country, endeavour to accommodate each other's point of view by means of discovering a *via media*. Indeed, the President was to serve as the ballast of the ship of the state to keep it on an even keel. In other words the Constitution provided for a system of checks and balances. The President had been granted reserve power to keep the Prime Minister and the political parties within the limits of the Constitution and to maintain correct balance between the Union on the one side and the States on the other. I submitted that note to President Dr. Rajendra Prasad. He perused it and then told me that the question of the powers of the President be kept pending. He was perhaps reluctant to pursue the question to avoid giving an impression that he was hungry for power and had ambitions of his own to play a determinative role in the political affairs of the country. But this passivity on his part, for whatever reason it may have been, would not stop the historical process which quite often decides political questions one way or the other.

THE ATTRITION OF CONSTITUTIONAL INSTITUTION

The tacit adoption of the doctrine of the finality of the advice of the Council of Ministers by most politicians, lawyers, journalists and even by the judges of the High Courts and the Supreme Court opened the way for the establishment of a veiled dictatorship of the then Union Prime Minister, Pt. Jawaharlal Nehru, impelled as he was by his ambition to transform India in conformity with his political and economic beliefs so that it may become a country of his dreams. He was in a hurry to achieve his objectives and was not to be restrained in his march by any Constitutional limitation when he was an ordinary citizen (but quite prominent in the political arena). He had contributed an article to the Modern review under a pseudonym Chanakya. In that article he had hinted that Jawaharlal should be watched for he has a dictatorial tendency. When he became the Prime Minster of the Union this dictatorial vein found expression in assuming the role of being the sole architect of future India. He could do so because of his political domination over the Congress Party but as stated above mainly because of the tacit adoption of the doctrine that the advice of the Council of Ministers (which in effect was advice of the Prime Minister only) was binding on the President of India in all circumstances and at all times. Not only that, Pt. Nehru was even impatient of the judgments of the

Supreme Court which interpreted the provisions of the Constitution that appeared to the Prime Minister, as regarding the administrative and political processes which the Prime Minister held to be essential for the realization of the India of his dreams. He observed that the judges appeared to be sitting in an Ivory tower. Thus he chafed at all kinds of Constitutional or political, or administrative constraints. He was, no doubt, inspired by the noblest sentiments but the endeavour to transform those sentiments into reality in a hurry led to dangerous consequences, which are being faced by the people of India today. The slide towards what may be termed as political nihilism had begun and continued with increasing acceleration. This became inevitable mainly, if not solely, because of the reduction of the President of India into a mere ceremonial but politically impotent figure.

One evil consequence, which had been anticipated by me was the misuse of the provisions of article 356. The misuse of that article started in the fifties of this century itself. It was used to solve the internecine rivalries and conflicts between the different factions of the Congress Party. Thus the tussle between G.C. Bhargava and Bhim Sen Sachar was stilled by the imposition of President's Rule in Punjab. But the most glaring misuse was in the case of the dismissal of the E.M.S. Namboodiripad (Communist) Ministry in Kerala. That Ministry had majority support in the Legislative Assembly of the State. An agitation led by the Nair Education Society against the Communist Ministry had assumed formidable dimensions. But it could not be honestly said that a situation had actually arisen in which the Government of the Kerala State could not be carried on in accordance with the provisions of the Constitution. In the Constitution there is a provision for preventive detention and the Code of Criminal Procedure 1898 which was then in force also provides for dealing with such civil disorders, so that agitation could have been successfully dealt with by the

Communist Ministry. The Congress Party in power at the Union level did not want the communist Ministry to continue in Kerala. So Dr. Rajendra Prasad, the President, was pressurized by Pt. Jawaharlal Nehru to impose President's rule by dismissing the Communist Ministry in power in Kerala State. It was a blatant partisan act on the part of the Congress Party. Dr. Rajendra Prasad is reported to have resisted the move but yielded to the insistence of the Prime Minister mainly because it was the prevailing doctrine that the advice of the Council of Ministers was binding. Thereafter, there have been umpteen cases of the dismissal of State Governments to achieve partisan ends. In the seventies of this century even a worse example was set by the Janata Government, when it practically coerced the acting President to dismiss the Congress Governments of all those States where the Congress party had failed to get even a single seat or had got only one or two seats at the General Election to the Lok Sabha held in 1977. It could not be said that because of that failure of the Congress Party a situation had arisen in those States in which the governments of those States could not be carried on in accordance with the provisions of the Constitution when the Congress Party came back into power in 1980 at the Union level, it repaid the compliment by securing the dismissal of the Janata Party Governments in the States where the Janata Party had been routed at the election to the Lok Sabha.

Another blatant misuse was of the provisions of Article 352 of the Constitution. Smt. Indira Gandhi was able to secure the signature of President Fakhruddin Ali Ahmed to the proclamation of Emergency under Article 352 of the Constitution in 1975 even though a situation had not arisen in which the safety of the Indian Polity was in imminent danger. She could induce the President to sign that proclamation, simply because the doctrine that the President was bound to act according to the advice tendered to him by the Union Council of Ministers, which for all practical purposes meant the advice of the union Prime Minister, had become a fixture in the minds of the elite and even of some of the incumbents of the office of President.

The dominance that Smt. Indira Gandhi came to have over party members in the Lok Sabha was also partly due to their apprehension that if they failed to abide by the wishes of the Prime Minister she could advise the President to dissolve the Lok Sabha. This situation again had arisen because of the doctrine of the binding nature of the advice of the Council of Ministers. Even the Ministers of the Council could not afford to disregard the wishes of the Prime Minister for the simple reason that their continuance as ministers depended on the pleasure of the Prime Minister on whose recommendation they had been appointed as ministers by the President and on whose recommendation they could be dismissed by the President. Thus the doctrine of the binding character of the ministerial advice to the President had made the Prime Minister the master of the members of her party and of the members of the Union Council of Ministers.

That was not all. The Governor of each Constituent State was to be appointed by the President, but by virtue of the above doctrine he (the President) had become a mere stamping instrument of the will of the Prime Minister. Thus the Prime Minister could get anyone appointed as the Governor of a Constituent State and also get him dismissed at his or her own sweet will. The Constitution had made provision for the Office of Governor to be the Kingpin for the running of the Government of the State in accordance with the provisions of the Constitution by giving him the power to recommend the dismissal of the State Government on the ground that it was not being carried on in accordance with the provisions of the Constitution. But this kingpin of the State became a mere instrument for carrying out the will of the Prime Minister of the Union. The Governor was to be the agent of the President in the State, but in actuality the Governor became a mere pliable tool in the hands of the Prime Minister of the Union. This position, however, had remained somewhat invisible during the period Pt. Jawaharlal Nehru remained the Prime Minister of the Union even though he had begun the practice of giving instructions couched as advice to the Governors of Constituent States through his periodical letters to them. From the strict Constitutional point of view he should have contacted the Governors of state only through the office of President for the simple reason that he was constitutionally empowered to deal only with the subjects in which the Union could act, and not to deal with the subjects exclusively entrusted by the Constitution to the States. This propriety was observed when the governors met in their annual conference. The President presided over such a conference and he addressed the Governors. The Prime Minister did come to that conference and answered the queries of the Governors. But he did not adopt the role of being their chief. But in the matter of sending epistles containing instruction in the form of advice he ignored this Constitutional propriety presumably because he felt that ultimately it was the Prime Minister who had to take care of all national interests as the real head of the Nation. But this practice of the Prime Minister did not raise any eyebrows of the elite because of the halo that surrounded the personality of Pt. Nehru as the leading figure in the freedom movement. The common people of course did not count in so far as the Constitutional proprieties were concerned. But the way Smt. Indira Gandhi used the office of the Governors of Constituent State to impose her imperious will on the Constituent States made it glaringly clear that the Governors had become pliable tools of her own Congress Party for doing whatever that Party and she herself wanted to be done in the Constituent States. Indeed the elected governments of those States, whether belonging to the Congress Party or even to other political parties opposed to the Congress could remain in office only so long as they continued to carry out the wishes of Smt. Indira Gandhi, the Union Prime Minister. The moment they displeased her, they incurred the danger of being thrown out of office by one stratagem or another. It also further meant that the people of any Constituent State did not count for much as again and again she got rid of the state governments she did not like.

The Federal character of the Indian Polity consequently came to be subverted notwithstanding the division of powers between the Union on one hand and the Constituent States on the other even though the federal character remained as an integral part of the Constitution. Such a situation could arise only because the President had been reduced to a cipher. It can be legitimately presumed that if the President as the Head of the Nation and the custodian of the interests of the Constituent States and the defender of the Constitution had not been tied down by that doctrine of the binding character of the advice of the Council of Ministers he would have not allowed such a situation to arise.

The power of appointment of judges of the Supreme Court and the High Court's came to be wielded by the Prime Minister of the Union by virtue of the employment of the doctrine of the binding character of the advice of the Union Council of Ministers which as stated above had in reality come to be the advice of the Prime Minister. The judiciary was contemplated by the Constitution to be independent of all control of the executive authorities of the Union and of the Constituent States so much so that even those who were to be appointed to be members of the lower judiciary could be appointed only on the recommendation of the High Court concerned or as a result of an open competitive examination held by the State Public Service Commission. It can be affirmed without any doubt that the Constitutional requirement was that the considerations of the interests of any political party were not to influence any decision in respect of the appointment of a judge of the High Court or the Supreme Court. This objective could be hoped to be realized only if a decision, for selecting a judge for appointment to the High Court or the Supreme Court, was taken by the President of India without being pressurised in any way by the leaders or managers of any political party. This implied that the party in power at the Union level in the case of the appointment of such judges should have no final say. But the above doctrine of the binding character of the ministerial advice enabled the Chief Minister of a State and the Prime Minister of the Union to become jointly the real appointing authority of the judges of the High Court of the concerned state and the Prime Minister as the sole appointing authority of the judges of the supreme Court in reality while the President was reduced to a mere stamping instrument of the decisions of the Prime Minister. Naturally, the Prime Minister of the Union in all cases of the appointment of a judge of the High Court of that State came to be in a position to subvert the independence of the judiciary by appointing, if they so willed, their pliant protégés in the Bar to the post of judges of such courts. When some judges of the Supreme Court pronounced a judgment, which the Prime Minister Smt. Indira Gandhi did not like she retaliated by superseding those judges when the appointment of the Chief Justice was made. The theory that judiciary should be a committed one, was also propounded by some of the leading aides of the Prime Minister. It was not stated by them in clear terms as to what the judges were to be committed to but their underlying view was that the commitment of the judges should be to the programme of the ruling party at the Union level presumably because the people of India had endorsed that programme by voting that party to power at the General Election to the Lok Sabha. In other words it was implicitly held by the party in power that in forming their judgment on the issues that came before them for adjudication the basic premise of the Supreme Court judges should be the central idea underlying the programme of the party in power. This should also be the case when exercising their power of judicial review. But it was not foreseen by such theorists, that for the judges of the Supreme Court to remain committed to the programme of the party ruling for the time being at the Union level, would land the Supreme Court into an impossible situation when the people of India threw out that party at the next General election. The Supreme Court was the creature of the Constitution and its commitment had to be to the Constitution only and not to any other political instrument if it was to maintain its character of a non-partisan arbiter in the affairs of the Indian people. Indeed one of the pillars of the democracy in India is the Supreme Court. But the adoption of the above mentioned doctrine of the binding character of ministerial advice at the Union level had given the Prime Minister of the Union the opportunity to undermine this pillar of democracy.

In this connection, it may be made clear that every political party and every brand of so called intellectuals in India were guilty of paving the way for the undermining of the democratic system as established by the Constitution of India by the dedication to what may be termed as British Political Unitarianism. It is indeed somewhat amazing that with all their intellectual acumen they failed to see the basic contradiction between the doctrine of Parliamentary supremacy which obtains in Great Britain and which in actual practice had come to mean the supremacy of the Prime Minister on the other. On the one hand most of them explicitly adhered to the principle of judicial review and on the other hand they expressed their loyalty to the doctrine of the binding character of the ministerial advice at the Union level. It is also amazing that in the matter of the determination of the age of a judge of High Court, the Supreme Court held that the Prime

Minister of the Union had absolutely no role to play and the file in that case should not have been sent to the Prime Minister because under the law the President of India alone had the authority to take a decision as to the age of a High Court judge. But in the matter of the appointment and transfer of judges of the High Courts, the Supreme Court in a way conceded that the Chief Minister of the concerned State and the Prime Minister of the Union had a deciding role to play and they could disregard the advice of the Chief Justice of the Supreme Court in the matter of the appointment of such judges. The determination of the age of a High Court judge is a minor matter as compared to the appointment of such a judge. But in the determination of that minor matter the court was not prepared to allow the Prime Minister of the Union any Constitutional power, while in the determination of such an important matter as the appointment of the judges of the High Court and the Supreme Court that court was prepared to give the Prime Minister a determining Constitutional role and had no compunction in treating the President as a stamping instrument in the hands of the Prime Minister. This adherence to the doctrine of the supremacy of the Prime Minister of the Union has led to the formulation of the view of the a National Front Government that in making recommendations for the appointment of High court and Supreme court judge, one consideration to be kept in view should be the due representation of the Scheduled Tribes, Scheduled Castes, women and the backward classes. In other words the principle of reservation is to be extended to the membership of the judicial office in the Supreme Court and the High Courts. The Constitution of India has made no provision for such reservation in the higher judiciary. It has laid down the qualifications for appointment of the judges of these courts and there is no provision for the relaxation of those qualifications in respect of the Scheduled Castes, Scheduled Tribes, Women and

Backward Classes. But once the sole consideration for the political parties becomes to garner votes by the adoption of every sort of tactics, howsoever, reprehensible the same may be from the viewpoint of National welfare, these parties would not baulk at the contamination of even the judicial system.

The misuse of the appointing power has been all pervasive. The appointment of the members of the Public Service Commissions has been reduced to the distribution of patronage to all sorts of persons. The Constitution makers did not lay down educational qualifications for appointment of the members of such commissions. It may be presumed that the very nature of the membership of such commissions implied that persons possessing high educational qualifications would alone be appointed as their members. In the case of the Union Public Service Commission the appointment of its member is to be made by the President of India and in the case of the State Public Service Commission, the appointment of its member is to be made by the Governor of the concerned States. These appointments are to be made in accordance with the provisions of Article 317 of the Constitution. But it may be presumed that in appointing the members of these Public Service Commission's, great care would be taken by the appointing authorities to appoint only persons possessing high educational qualifications for the simple reason that such members will be selecting persons to the civil services of the Union or the civil services of the state as the case may be, and would be making such selections from amongst candidates who would be possessing educational qualifications prescribed for the posts to be filled. Normally, such qualifications for the Class I Administrative Service of the Union or of every state would at least be the possession of a graduate degree in the prescribed subjects. Naturally, it could have been presumed that the person to be appointed as a member of the Union or State Public Service Commission shall at best have an educational qualification, which was required to be possessed by a candidate for the Class I Service of the Union or the State. But as the President and the State Governor were reduced to be mere stamping instruments in the hands of the Prime Minister of the Union and the Chief Minister of the concerned State, as the case may be, the Minister of the Cabinet at both the Union and State level who had been allotted the business of making such appointments was able to appoint the protégés of the political party in power as members of such Public Service commissions notwithstanding that such protégés did not possess educational qualifications which were required to be possessed by the candidates for even Class II service of the Union or the State concerned. What was still more reprehensible was that persons of doubtful integrity were appointed to such Public Service Commissions with the consequence that at present a number of State Public Service Commissions are alleged to be hotbeds of corruption, or to have become a sort of an extension unit of the political party in power. Thus the fountain from which originated the civil service of the State became polluted. The Union Public Service Commission has not suffered that kind of deterioration but if the dominance of the political parties and their chiefs continued further there is every possibility that the commission may also suffer deterioration in its standard.

The union bureaucracy has been exposed to the evil machinations of the political bosses because of the inordinate power the latter have begun to exercise in the sphere of administration. During the regime of the erstwhile British rulers the bureaucrats were shielded from adverse actions of the political bosses in as much as the Governor had the power by law to provide them special protection. But now that the Governor of the State has been denuded of all power as a result of the adoption of the doctrine of the binding character of ministerial advice, the bureaucrats have been directly exposed to the favour and frowns of their political bosses. A bureaucrat who has been subjected to some injustice in the matter of his service interests can no doubt have recourse to administrative tribunals. But even that recourse does not afford much relief on account of the delay that inevitably occurs in the pronouncing of its judgment by the Administrative Tribunal after a due hearing of the case. But the weapon of frequent transfers can be and is utilized by the political boss to break down even the firmest bureaucrat and make him implement even the most illegitimate, if not wholly illegal, demands of the political boss. The position has been reached in which even the ordinary members of the ruling party can procure the transfer of a bureaucrat who does not accede to the illegitimate demands of that member of that party. Thus the main function of the bureaucracy of carrying on the administration in accordance with the Constitution and the law has been practically stultified.

The reduction of the President to a mere instrument for the registration of the will of the Union Council of Ministers enabled the Prime Minister of the Union to fiddle with the Constitution itself. The fathers of the Constitution had sought to ensure that the Constitution could not be amended whenever it appeared to a powerful political leader that it was an obstacle in his having his way in the economic or legislative sphere. Article 368 as originally enacted by the Constituent Assembly implied that an amendment of the Constitution was to be effected by the Parliament acting as a constituent assembly and not as a mere legislative body. In chapter 2 of Part 5 of the Constitution, elaborate provision has been made for the Constitution of the Union Legislature, its officials and the procedure that has to be followed for the transaction of its legislative business. What is material in contrast to the process for the amendment of the Constitution is the process laid down for the enactment of ordinary laws. It is provided that a legislative Bill is to be passed by the

Majority of the members present and voting in each House, but in the event of the two houses failing to agree in respect of any legislative Bill, a joint session of the two Houses can be summoned for the consideration of that Bill and for passing or rejecting it by a majority of the members present and voting in that joint session. The Bill so passed is then to be presented to the President for his assent and he may assent to the same, or withhold his assent. But in the case of an amendment to the Constitution the amending Bill has to be passed by each House of the Union Parliament sitting separately and that also by the Majority of the total membership of each House and by a two thirds majority of the members present and voting in each House. It was then to be presented to the President for his assent unless it was a Bill to which the proviso to Article 368 applied. In that case the Amending Constitution Bill had to be approved by the legislatures of at least half of the Constituent States by resolutions approving the Bill before it could be presented to the President for his assent. The President by virtue of his oath to preserve, protect and defend the Constitution could give his assent to such Constitution amendment or withhold his assent. In this matter he would have been acting not as the head of the Union Executive but as an integral unit of what could be termed as a law making body, consisting of the Lok Sabha, the Rajya Sabha and the President each acting independently in the manner prescribed by Article 368 and in the case of a Constitution Amendment Bill to which proviso to Article 368 applied, as also of the legislatures of the Constituent States. It has been an unfortunate practice of political leaders, and even of jurists and judges to take the two Houses of Parliament as the totality of that body. But such a practice is based on ignoring the specific provision of Article 79 of the Constitution. That article specifically provides that the (Union) "Parliament shall consist of the President and two Houses". The President is thus an inseparable and integral unit of Parliament separately from the two Houses. Thus the assent of the President to a legislative measure is as essential to a Bill as its being passed by the two houses of Parliament before it can become an 'Act of Parliament'. The Parliament is thus like a three wheeled vehicle for the passage of any law. In Great Britain the monarch ceased to be an effective and working third wheel of the legislative machine on account of the peculiar historical circumstances of the country and to a great extent for the reason that the continuance of monarchy became wholly dependent on the will of the House of Commons. But in India those historical conditions did not exist at any time and the continuance of the office of the President did not depend on the sweet will of the Lok Sabha or even both the Houses. Provisions of Article 368, as originally framed, did not give the power of amending Article 54 to the two Houses of Parliament alone but made it essential that such an amendment had to be approved by the legislatures of at least half of the Constituent States. It has been explained above that there was every probability that a party that was opposed to the party ruling at the Union level may be in power in more than half the Constituent State. So any amendment of the Constitution for the abolition of the office of President had no chance of being duly enacted even if the President was to be kept out of reckoning. But once it became the ruling doctrine that the President of India was nothing more than a replica of the British Monarch, and that he was bound to act in accordance with whatever advice was tendered to him by the Union Council of Ministers, which in practical reality meant the advice of the Prime Minister of the Union, the Constitution itself came to be exposed to the will and machinations of the Prime Minister of the Union. He could treat it in quite a number of cases as a football to be kicked in any direction at his sweet will. The proviso to Article 368 of the Constitution could be made ineffective in actual practice by the Prime Minister of the Union. He could do this by undertaking the amendment of the Constitution when a state of emergency had been proclaimed and existed. Smt. Indira Gandhi was able to get a far reaching amendment of the Constitution including an amendment of Article 368 itself enacted in 1975 after she had, by her own action, brought into existence a state of emergency and that also to save her own position as the Prime Minister when her election to the Lok Sabha had been set aside by the High Court of Allahabad and she had been disqualified to be a member of the Lok Sabha for a period of six years.

There have been frequent occasions when the Council of Ministers under the imperious direction of the Prime Minister of the Union took executive decisions or got legislation passed by the two Houses of Parliament and assented to by the President which had to be knocked down by the Supreme Court. Thus a kind of hostility towards the Supreme Court developed amongst the leaders of the Congress who were in power at the Union level during the last forty years. This is not good for the health of the Indian Polity. Again Smt. Indira Gandhi made the Union Council of Ministers take a decision to abolish the privy purses of the erstwhile rulers of the princely States. These rulers had acceded to the Indian Union on the understanding that was completely repudiated by the Union Council of Ministers by getting legislation enacted for the abolition of the privy purses of the princes. It appears that this violation of the understanding with the princes is to some extent responsible for the hostility of a section of Sikhs towards the Union of India. Not much need be said about the misuse of the provisions of Article 356 by the Union Council of Ministers and the Prime Minister of the Union. If the President had been able to disregard the advice of the Council of Ministers in such cases, then India would not be in the sorry position in which we find it today.

As shown above dangerous developments and the

attrition of the institutions of the Indian polity have taken place because of the doctrine of the absolutely binding character of the advice of the council of ministers having been maintained by the politicians, jurists, judges and the members of the fourth Estate all along during the last forty years. Nearly all of them have been led to adopt that course partly because of their tacit belief that the Constitutional precedents and conventions of Great Britain were basic features of the Cabinet system of government and are, therefore, applicable to India in the same way and to the same extent as they apply in Great Britain.

The apprehension entertained by the English speaking members of the Indian elite that if the President of India were to have the power of using his discretion in the discharge of his functions, then there was the likelihood that an ambitious politician elected to the office of the President would have the opportunity to establish his dictatorship in the country and to subvert the Constitution has also prompted them to adhere to that doctrine. In their view the President was not directly responsible to the elected representatives of the people whereas the Council of Ministers and the Prime Minister remained continuously accountable to the elected representatives of the people in the matter of the exercise of all their functions and could be dismissed by the Lok Sabha by means of a simple vote of no confidence. As against this the removal of the President from his office by means of impeachment for acting in violation of the Constitution can be secured only by means of a resolution passed by the investigating house by a two thirds majority of the total membership of that house. Such a two thirds majority would be extremely difficult to secure. Indeed even the preliminary step for the process of impeachment to commence can be taken only with the approval of two-thirds majority of the total membership of the House in which the resolution for the initiation of the process for impeachment has been moved.

Even that two thirds majority would be extremely difficult if not impossible, to secure. Thus in their view it is almost impossible to enforce accountability of the President to the popular will, in so far as the discharge of his functions under the Constitution are concerned. In other words, to allow the President the power to act in accordance with his discretion or individual judgment is to open the way for the establishment of Presidential dictatorship or to political paralysis as a direct consequence of the perennial disputes between the Council of Ministers on the one hand and the President on the other. Either of the two developments would amount to political suicide in so far as the people of India are concerned.

The above view in respect of the Presidential discretion being pregnant with the above mentioned dangers appears at first sight to be quite reasonable and acceptable. But if the question is examined minutely it would be found to have a considerable element of fallacy.

It rests on the basic premise that the Constitutional accountability of the Chief of the Council of Ministers namely the Prime Minister to popular will is practically enforceable while that of the President is practically unenforceable. But is this premise maintainable? To answer this question we must first keep in view the undeniable truth that no political Constitution is a self-enforcing magic or miracle. By itself and in itself it is just an invocation to the people of the concerned country to conduct their group affairs harmoniously keeping constantly in view the basic objectives they are seeking to achieve in their group life. But this invocation must find sympathetic resonance continuously in the hearts of the politically active and vigilant segment of the population of the country, as also receive silent acquiescence of those segments of the population which do not have any hankering for the acquisition of the power to impose their will on others to make the latter conduct their personal affairs in compliance with the formers will but remain content with the pursuit of their own interests largely connected with their existence as human beings. In other words the degree of the enforceability of the Constitution is directly proportional to the intensity and extensiveness of the feeling amongst the members of the population that the Constitution is the channel within which the life of the groups and individuals can continuously and smoothly flow to ensure their spiritual and physical well-being. But while the Constitution is a channel it is also a fetter on the freewheeling and dealings of those who are in a position to indulge in the same. Thus in every community there is a straining at the margins of the Constitution by those who are in a hurry to effect drastic changes in the economic or creedal spheres of group life of the country. In India this phenomenon may be anticipated to occur much more frequently than in countries the group life or which is comparatively much more homogenous or settled. In view of the size and heterogeneity of its population, there are bound to be in India severe social or group tensions and consequent straining at the Constitution. The question which, therefore, has to be faced is as to who between the Prime Minister of the Union on the one hand and the President of India on the other hand shall have greater inclination and urge to rush on to accomplish what he considers to be absolutely necessary for the solution of the problems the country is faced within its internal affairs and external relations even if his actions are not in accordance with the spirit of the Constitution even though by some stretching the same may be held to be conformable to what appears to be its literary form. The answer to that question can only be that it would be the Prime Minister of the Union of India and not the President. The simple reason for this observation is that the Prime Minister of the initiator of various kinds of programme for the channelising the energies of the Indian people for economic and cultural advancement whereas the President of India has the negative role of checking any rash action of the political party in power at the Union level which would evidently lead to the attrition of the Constitution of India. The oath or affirmation for preserving, protecting and defending the Constitution and the law, which the President has to subscribe to before assuming his office lays, to repeat again, an obligation on him to perform that negative role. It is only in the matter of the exercise of his reserve and extra ordinary power of proclaiming a state of emergency or of assuming the governance of a Constituent State in the event of a situation arising in the state in which it is impossible to carry on the government of that state in accordance with the provisions of the Constitution that he is empowered to take an initiative in the matter even though such initiative remains conditioned by the advice of the Council of Ministers and controlled by the two Houses of Parliament wherein the Council of Ministers ex hypothesi has controlling voice. Thus the President has a limited and negative role. Consequently, there can be hardly any occasion for the President to take any action for which the question of his personal accountability would arise. As against that every action of the Prime Minister as the leading and controlling figure of the Council of Ministers shall be pregnant with fateful consequences for the people of India mainly on account of the powers allotted to the Union by the Constitution. Naturally, he has to remain accountable for all his actions to the Indian people. If the governing apparatus of the Union were to be compared to an automobile, then the Council of Ministers and the Prime Minister, with their control over the two houses of Parliament may be compared to the Propulsion system while the role of the Presidential Office would be that of an emergency braking system. It can no doubt be urged that even the application of Constitutional breaks may be a means of flouting the will of the people and a road to the ultimate establishment of a sort of dictatorship. But such a possibility is extremely remote in the conditions within which the President has to abjure partisan policies before he can hope to secure the support of those who rule the Union as also of those who rule the Constituent States. On election to the President's office he has to renounce the membership of the political party of which he may have been a member. A person having an ambition to play a significant role in the arena of active policies would not covet the office of the President, and in any case would not be able to win an election to that office. It is only a person who has become satiated with partisan politics and seeks to serve the people of India by retiring from the amphitheater of partisan politics who would seek to move into the Presidential office where he can be the ballast to keep the ship of state on an even keel. So there need not be any serious apprehension of any danger of the President using his limited and reserve discretion arbitrarily. The difficulty of enforcing his accountability should not, therefore, be given crucial importance. The danger of misuse of power by the Prime Minister on the contrary is quite real in the situation in which the office of the President has been reduced to impotence. As the head of the Council of Ministers the Prime Minister has a stranglehold over the members of that council. As leader of the majority party in the Lok Sabha and having the power to ask for the dissolution of that Sabha, the Prime Minister has a stranglehold over the Lok Sabha. Rajya Sabha also can be reduced to a powerless body by the Prime Minister of the Union by virtue of the limitless power of patronage and by the summoning of the joint session of the two Houses of Parliament in the event of the Rajya Sabha trying to block any piece of legislation which the Prime Minister is determined to enact. As explained hereinbefore the Prime Minister can also neutralize the judiciary. Thus the Prime Minister has all the potential to establish what may be termed as plebiscitary dictatorship. In this connection it would not be inappropriate to refer to the attitude of contempt, which

Smt. Indira Gandhi adopted towards the judgment of the Allahabad High Court on being disqualified to hold office by that court. To her the verdict of the populace was alone acceptable and she referred to the verdict of courts as a laughable joke. She was able to adopt that attitude largely because she had a belief that she had freed herself from any control by the President by securing an amendment of Article 74 to the effect that the President was bound to abide by the advice of the Council of Ministers. In 1950 that article did not have that provision and yet the jurists, and the politicians and the members of the fourth Estate all parroted as stated hereinbefore the slogan that the President was bound to act in accordance with the advice of the Council of Ministers.

It is interesting to note that notwithstanding the general view that under Article 74 as originally enacted by the Constituent Assembly the advice of the Council of Ministers was binding on the President and consequently the President has no role except a purely formal one, in the governance of the country, Smt. Indira Gandhi out of her apprehension that there was a possibility that the advice of the Council of Ministers may not be treated by a President as binding on him, got an amendment made in 1975 in Article 74 of the Constitution for inserting therein an expression to the effect that the President shall act in accordance with that advice. Evidently, her belief was that by means of that amendment the advice of the Council of Ministers had become binding on the President in all circumstances and at all times. But if that was to be the effect of that amendment, then it was absolutely necessary that a consequential amendment was also made in clause (2) of Article 103 of the Constitution to ensure that in the matter of the disqualification having been incurred by any member of the two House of Parliament, the advice of the Council of Ministers tendered to the President shall be binding. But as no such amendment was, or could be made in that clause so it can be inferred that when amending

Article 74, it was understood by all concerned and also by the Union that there are certain areas in which the President is not bound to take the advice of the Council of Ministers. In this connection it may be added that the Constituent Assembly was fully conscious of the necessity of fair and free elections being held to the Houses of Parliament as also to the legislatures of the Constituent States if the democratic government they were setting up was to function as a true representative of the Indian People. In other words that Assembly was conscious that the Union Executive should not be armed to be able to act in partisan manner in some Constitutional fields and that in those fields the Council of Ministers of the Union should not be able to impose its will on the President.

It would appear that the functioning of the Indian Democracy during the last forty years, certain matters have cropped up in which the question of the Union Council of Ministers tendering their advice to the President does not arise. For instance, if a petition is submitted to the President for granting his sanction for the prosecution of the Prime Minister of the Union for the members of his family, then there can be no question of the Council of Ministers tendering their advice to the President in regard to the grant of the sanction for the prosecution of the Prime Minister. Indeed some jurists have occasionally been approaching the President with a request to take action independently of the advice of the Council of Ministers or even contrary to that advice. Recently, in respect of a mercy petition submitted to the President by a person whom the Supreme Court had convicted of such as heinous offence as murder and sentenced him to be hanged, it was urged by an eminent lawyer that the President had the power to examine the record of the case and form an opinion as to whether there had been a miscarriage of justice due to non-production of a material piece of evidence and on the basis of that examination the President could commute the sentence of death to one for life imprisonment. This necessarily implied that in his view the President could be able to exercise his discretion in the matter of the commutation of a sentence pronounced by a court of justice and that the President could do so in disregard of the advice of the concerned minister in respect of the grant or rejection of the mercy petition of the applicant. There have been frequent occasions when politicians have approached the President to take a decision as to which party commands a majority in the lower House of Union Legislature. Petitions have been submitted to the President for the grant of sanction for the prosecution of the person holding the office of the Prime Minister of the Union. Obviously, the President cannot be expected to act in accordance with the advice of the Council of Ministers in the matter of the granting or rejecting such a petition. Those who submit such a petition obviously hold the view that the President does have the power to exercise his discretion in taking a decision in respect of such a petition. Thus it appears that a realization is dawning upon a certain segment of the political and legal elite that there can be situations, in which the President should be able to exercise his discretion or individual judgment independently of the advice of the Council of Ministers or even in disregard of that advice, notwithstanding the provisions of Article 74 as it stands today. Even then the effect of Article 74 as it stands today on the question of what role, if any, the President can Constitutionally perform needs careful examination.

संविधान की जानकारी आम लोगों तक पहुंचाने की जरूरत पर जोर

नई दिल्ली, २७ अक्तूबर (जनसत्ता) । संविधान सभा के सदस्यों की बैठक में आज यह राय जाहिर की गई कि राष्ट्रपति शासन पद्धति पर चर्चा न हो । एम. निज़लिंगप्पा ने तो कहा कि बैठक में इस मुद्दे पर चर्चा होना गलत होगा । लिहाजा फैसला किया गया कि बैठक में शामिल २१ सदस्यों को इसकी जानकारी दे दी जानी चाहिए ।

यह काम किया संविधान सभा के पूर्व अंडर सेक्रेटरी बाल कृष्ण ने, उन्होंने कहा कि अमेरिकी शासन पद्धति के राष्ट्रपति और विधायिका अलग अलग है ।

फ्रांस में द' गाल ने जो पद्धति लागू की उसमें राष्ट्रपति केबिनेट को भंग कर सकता है, संसद बर्खास्त कर सकता है और जब, जो चाहे फैसला ले सकता है । उन्होंने कहा कि निजी तौर पर वे भारत में लागू पद्धति के हिमायती हैं ।

वे सदस्यों की इस बात से सहमत थे कि भारत को संघीय गणराज्य होना चाहिए और राज्यों को आज की तुलना में ज्यादा अधिकार मिलने चाहिएं ।

सदस्यों ने आज संविधान की आम लोगों को जानकारी देने के मुद्दे पर चर्चा भी की । उन्होंने कहा कि इसे सर्वोच्च प्राथमिकता दी जानी चाहिए ।

डा. एम.एस. मेहता ने कहा कि लोगों को संविधान के तहत अपने अधिकारों व जिम्मेदारियों की जानकारी होनी चाहिए । उन्होंने राष्ट्रीय एकता को विशेष महत्व दिए जाने पर भी जोर दिया ।

सभी सदस्यों ने कहा कि सर्वोच्च प्राथमिकता देश को नरक में जाने से बचाने की अहम समस्या पर दी जानी चाहिए । यह समस्या सार्वजनिक जीवन में नैतिक पतन की है । जब तक इसे नहीं सुलझा लिया जाता, कोई समस्या हल नहीं हो सकती ।

संविधान सभा के कुल ६५ सदस्य जीवित हैं । इनमें से २१ आज की बैठक में शामिल हुए ।

बैठक में यह भी सुझाव दिया गया कि प्रधानमंत्री श्रीमती गांधी को यह सलाह दी जाए कि प्रधानमंत्री या राष्ट्रपति के चित्र कहां कहां लगाए जाएं ।

सदस्य सोमवार को केंद्र-राज्यों संबंधों पर बने सरकारिया आयोग से मिलेंगे ।

News item in a Hindi newspaper about meeting of surviving members of the Constituent Assembly.

PRESIDENTS ROLE

Article 74 occurs in Chapter I of Part V of the Constitution. That part contains provisions relating to the Constitution of the Union. It is divided into a number of chapters. Chapter I relates to the Executive of the Union. Chapter II sets out the Constitution of the Union Legislature. Chapter III relates to the legislative powers of the President. Chapter IV sets out the Constitution of the Union Judiciary. Chapter V deals with the appointment, power, functions etc. of the Attorney General of India. It is obvious from this scheme of Part V of the Constitution that the fathers of the Constitution were proceeding to some extent at least on the principle of separation of powers. They did not make a watertight separation of the executive from the Legislature as they made provision for the Council of Ministers to be the hyphen that joins and the buckle that fastens the Union Executive with Union Legislature. But the fact that they considered it expedient to insert Article 74 to 78 in the chapter relating to the Executive of the Union may be taken to imply that Article 74 related mainly and principally with the Union Executive. That article does not provide for the powers and functions of the Council of Ministers. It only makes a mandatory provision for the existence of a Council of Ministers to aid and advise the President in the exercise of his functions. It may be inferred that the reference to the President in that Article actually refers to him as the head of the Union Executive and not to him as a constituent element of the Union Legislature. As the embodiment of the Union Executive he would be exercising the functions, which the President as the Union Executive would be discharging. So even though the term 'Executive' has not been used to qualify the expression 'functions' occurring in that Article, it can be taken to qualify that expression by virtue of that Article being part of the chapter relating to the Union Executive in Chapter 2. The term President, wherever it occurs may be taken to refer to the President as an integral element of the Union Legislature, that is to say being the third component of the Union legislature along with but separate from the other two components thereof namely the Lok Sabha and the Rajya Sabha. In chapter 3 of that part the President, in exercise of his Legislative power, has been given the power to issue ordinances when the two houses of the Union Legislature are not in session and the President is satisfied that a situation exists in which it is necessary to make appropriate legislation to meet that situation without any delay. But such an ordinance, being a legislative measure, has to be approved by the two Houses of the Union Legislature on their being summoned to meet, and the ordinance ceases to be in force if it is not approved by the two Houses within the time prescribed therefor. The satisfaction of the President in respect of the necessity of the promulgation of an ordinance is his satisfaction as an integral element of the Union Legislature and not as the embodiment of the Union Executive. In other words the President is not bound to issue an ordinance whenever the Union Council of Ministers advises him to promulgate an ordinance. He must be personally satisfied that a situation does exist which requires that an immediate legislative measure must be promulgated to meet that situation. In other words, the provision of Article 74 come to have limited operation in the matter of the promulgation of ordinances and that also because the Council of Ministers has been made a directing and controlling committee of the Union Legislature specifically by the Constitution of India. In this respect it may be pointed out that the Cabinet in Great Britain came to be a kind of controlling committee of the two Houses of Parliament by means of the evolution of Constitutional conventions and only at a very late stage a reference to the Cabinet came to be incorporated in law. But in India the Constitution has made a specific provision about the joint responsibility of the Council of Ministers to the Lok Sabha and about the requirement that no person may remain a member of the council of minister beyond a period of six months unless he becomes a member of either House of the Union Parliament before the expiry of the said period of six months. This implied that normally the members of the Council of Ministers have to be members of either House of Parliament. Thus the Council of Ministers constitutes a sort of Central Committee of the two houses even though it is not so termed. Thus it is by virtue of the Council of Ministers being a kind of a directing and controlling committee of the two Houses of Parliament that it comes to be a key figure in the legislative process of the union. It is in that capacity that it takes the initiative in formulating legislative measures and piloting them in the two Houses of Union Parliament. It is in that capacity that it places before the President the drafts of the ordinances, which it wants to be promulgated. But the President as an integral element of the Union legislature must be satisfied of the urgent necessity of the promulgation of such an ordinance. This satisfaction of the President shall be his own and not that of the Council of Ministers. If that were not to be the case then this power of the promulgation of ordinances can be misused to short circuit the legislative process laid down by the Constitution for the enactment of laws and to emasculate the union legislature. A similar provision relating to the promulgation of ordinances by the Governors of the Constituent States has been grossly misused by the Council of Ministers of the concerned States mainly because the distinction between the Governor as the Chief Executive of the state and the Governor as an integral element of the legislature of the concerned state has not been kept in view and it has been taken for granted that the Governor is bound to abide with whatever advice is tendered to him by the Council of Ministers of the concerned state. If the above mentioned distinction had been kept in view then it would not have been possible for the Council of Ministers of any state to misuse the power of promulgating ordinances. If we are to eliminate any future possibility of the misuse of the power of promulgating ordinances at the Union level then this distinction between the capacity of the President as the Chief Union Executive and his capacity as an integral element of the Union legislature must continually be kept in view. If that is done then the provisions of Article 74 as it stands after the Forty Second amendment of the Constitution would not compel the President as an integral element of the Union Legislature to abide by the advice of the Council of Ministers in all circumstances in the matter of the promulgation of ordinances. This does not mean that even if the Council of Ministers puts forward facts that would satisfy any reasonable person of the necessity of the promulgation of an appropriate legislative measure to meet a challenging situation which has arisen when the two Houses of Parliament are not in session, the President shall be competent to refuse to promulgate the legislative measure recommended by the Council of Ministers. What is being urged is only that the President must be satisfied of the necessity of the promulgation of the recommended ordinance. No President who remains loyal to the oath of his office will act arbitrarily in the matter.

Apart from the dangerous possibility of the misuse of the power of promulgating ordinances undeniably there has been gross misuse of the power of the declaration of emergency as also the power of dismissing the elected

Government of the Constituent States and the establishment of the Presidents rule therein. This misuse became possible, as above said, because the term 'President' occurring in Article 352 to 360 of the Constitution was taken to mean the President as the Chief Executive of the Union. But from the context of those articles it would appear that the term President occurring therein implies the President as the elected representative of both the Union and the States. The Constitution has made a division of powers between the Union on the one side and the Constituent States on the other. The powers allotted to the Constituent States are Executive, legislative and Judicial in character and are to be exercised by the concerned States independently of the Union except the few cases specifically set out by the Constitution. Thus under normal conditions the Union has its exclusive sphere wherein it may exercise its powers and similarly the Constituent States have their exclusive sphere wherein they may exercise their powers. Keeping in view the conditions prevailing in India, the Constitution makers considered it expedient to make effective Constitutional provisions for the maintenance and preservation of the integrity and longevity of the Indian Polity, which may be threatened by external invasion or internal insurrection. But these provision had to be exercised while keeping the national interests and not partisan interests in view.

It may not be denied that in terms of the provisions of the Constitution the Union Government as also the State Governments are to be run by political parties. These parties no doubt profess to be wedded to the promotion on national interests but the stark reality is that each political party seeks to promote what are held by it to be measures conducive to keep it in the seat of power. Thus each political party comes to have vested partisan interests, which it cannot but promote at all costs. Thus the political party in power at the Union level has its own vested partisan interests, which it cannot afford to neglect if it seeks to maintain its continued and united existence. It is, therefore, evident that notwithstanding all its devotion to national interests, the Union Council of Ministers (consisting as it does of members of a Political Party) would not exercise this power of suspending the division of powers made by the Constitution between the Union and the Constituent States remaining wholly free from Partisan considerations. In any case those adversely affected by the suspension of the said division of powers cannot be expected to accept that the Union Council of Ministers has acted solely in national interest in resorting to that suspension of the division of powers. It is therefore reasonable, as argued before, that this reserve power should be exercised solely by the President who is at once the representative of the Union and also of the Constituent States, who does not have any partisan interests to preserve and promote and who can be seen to have acted in national interest.

This does not mean that the Union Council of Ministers has no role whatever to play in this matter. The division of power made by the Constitution does indicate that the preservation of the unity, integrity and safety of the country are matters in which the Union Council of Ministers have to play a key role. Defence, communications and foreign affairs including the declaration of war and entering into peace, which are of crucial importance for the unity and integrity of Indian are vested in the Union Executive. Naturally the union Council of Ministers and its leader namely the Prime Minister has necessarily to place before the President the facts on the basis of which the President shall feel satisfied that a situation has arisen in the state in which the government thereof cannot be carried on in accordance with the provisions of the Constitution of India. But what is urged is merely that the Union Council of Ministers and the Union Prime Minister cannot and, in any case, should not claim that the President is Constitutionally bound to dismiss the elected Government of a Constituent State merely because the said Council or the Prime Minister believes that a situation has arisen in the state in which the Government thereof cannot be carried on in accordance with the provisions of the Constitution. The President, as the custodian of the interest of the Constituent States by virtue of his oath of office as also by virtue of having been a choice of the Constituent States, has necessarily to satisfy himself as to whether the recommendation for the dismissal of the Government of the concerned Constituent State made by the Union Council of Ministers or the Union Prime Minister is based on indisputable facts and circumstances, which reveal that in actuality a situation has arisen in which the Government of the concerned Constituent State cannot be carried on in accordance with the provisions of the Constitution.

There can be no reason to apprehend that the President will not give due respect and consideration to what the Council of Minister and /or the Prime Minister has recommended. After all the President would be a responsible statesman and would be conscious that the governance of the country has to be carried on with the cooperation and goodwill of the Council of Ministers and /or the Prime Minister. He would also be aware that the people of India expect him and the Council of Ministers to act in harmony in the matter of the governance of the country. The emphasis on his duty to personally satisfy himself as to the claim being made that there is a breakdown of the Constitutional machine in a Constituent State is being made firmly only to ensure that it may not be possible for the Union Council of Ministers and /or the Union Prime Minister to bring about the dismissal of an elected Government of a constituent state with the sole object of promoting their own partisan interests. The fathers of the Constitution did not visualize that in this extremely delicate matter any action would be taken by the Union Executive in a partisan spirit. They were inserting the emergency provisions as a matter of abundant caution to be used only if and when there did occur a breakdown of the Constitutional machinery in a Constituent State or the safety of India was in fact endangered by external aggression or internal insurrection. Unfortunately, however, my apprehension of these provisions being misused for promoting partisan interests did come to be borne out by the developments that took place after 1950. It is now recognised that the provisions of Article 356 have been misused by union Council of Ministers and even by the Union Prime Minister acting in his own discretion.

Notwithstanding what has been said above it cannot be denied that on account of the amendment made in Article 74 by inserting therein a provision to the effect that the President shall act in accordance with the advice tendered to him by the Council of Ministers (which as shown herein ultimately means the advice of the Prime Minister) the Constitutional situation in this matter has become somewhat more delicate. There cannot be any escape from the Constitutional position that the Union Council of Ministers and /or the Prime Minister shall have the right to tender their advice to the President in the matter of desirability of the dismissal of the elected Government of a Constituent State in which in their view a situation has arisen in which the governance of the state cannot be carried on in accordance with the provisions of the Constitution. There may even be a situation in which, the Union Council of Ministers and /or the Union Prime Minister hold the view that the governments of a number of Constituent States have ceased to have the mandate of the electorate to rule those States as has become evident in their party being completely routed at the General Election held for the Lok Sabha and as such have no Constitutional right to remain in the seat of power in those constituent States and must therefore, be dismissed and fresh elections to the assemblies of those States be held, and accordingly advise the President to dismiss those Governments, dissolve their Legislative Assemblies and take over the governance of those States in his own hands. In such a situation what has the President to do?

THE PRINCIPAL

BIRLA COLLEGE
PILANI, JAIPUR STATE.

Dated AUGUST 23, 196 .

    Prof. Bal Krishna, M.A. (History), M.A. (Politics) worked for full four years as professor and head of the department of History and Politics in the Birla College. He came to us in 1942 with a brilliant academic record of which any scholar can be proud and with several years' experience of teaching in the Meerut College.

    It is a pleasure for me to testify to the thorough knowledge of his subject, the command over language (Hindi & English), the power of clear analysis and lucid exposition which combine to make Prof. Bal Krishna a very fine and stimulating lecturer. The numerous discussions I have had with him on literature, philosophy, religion, politics and education impressed me deeply with a sense of his clear grasp of fundamentals and his wide-ranging knowledge and study.

    Prof. Bal Krishna took a leading part in building up the academic life of the College. He acted for three years as professor-in-charge of the College library and worked hard to organise it efficiently. He was throughout the period of his stay here the Speaker of the Students' Parishad and guided it with firmness and tact. For one year before his departure he was in charge of a big, new hostel, and showed considerable administrative ability in organising it.

    I am sorry Prof. Bal Krishan left the College at the end of the session 1946-47 for better prospects elsewhere. I wish him all success and happiness in his new field of activity, but the Birla College is poorer today by his departure. *He will be an asset to any university or university college.*

S. Dal
M.A., B.T.
PRINCIPAL

Such a recommendation would be obviously unconstitutional because what the Constitution provides is that action under Article 356 can be taken only when a situation has arisen in the state in which the governance of the Constituent State cannot, actually, be carried on in accordance with the provisions of the Constitution. The Constitution does not provide that if a political party has failed to secure seats in a General Election to the Lok Sabha held after some time has elapsed after the General Election to the Legislative Assembly had been held and at which that political party had secured a majority of seats in the Legislative Assembly of that state, then on account of its defeat at the subsequent General Election to the Lok Sabha it shall be deemed that a situation has arisen in the state in which the Government of the State by that political party cannot be carried on in accordance with the provisions of the Constitution. Does Article 74 imply that the President is bound to act in accordance with a patently unconstitutional advice of the Union Council of Ministers and /or of the Union Prime Minister? Can it be legitimately urged that the President merely because the Union Council of Ministers and /or the Union Prime Minister has stated that a situation has arisen in which the Governments of a number of Constituent States cannot be considered to have the mandate of the electorate to rule over those States and have therefore recommended that the Government of those States be dismissed and the legislative assemblies of those States dissolved, is bound to state that he is satisfied that the Government of those States cannot be carried on in accordance with the provisions of the Constitution, even though he has had no occasion to apply his mind to the actual conditions obtaining in those States. It is submitted that to urge that the President has no option but to implement such a recommendation of the Union Council of Ministers and /or the Union Prime Minister would mean the deletion of any reference to the satisfaction of the President in Article 356. It would then read as if it was provided therein that on the recommendation of the Union Council of Ministers, the President may by a proclamation that a situation has arisen in which the Government of a State cannot be carried in accordance with the Constitution, take over

(a) The Governance of the particular Constituent State(s)

(b) Dissolve the Legislative Assembly of the Constituent State(s).

Such an implied amendment of Article 356 on the basis of what is provided for in Article 74 as it presently stands after the Forty Second Constitutional Amendment is not permissible.

One reason for this view is that the term 'advice' in article 74 does not include 'unconstitutional advice'. It is evident *ipso facto* that the Union Council of Ministers and /or the Union Prime Minister are required to act only in accordance with the provisions of the Constitution as their own position and the powers they exercise are derived from the Constitution itself. So the advice they tender to the President must be in conformity to the letter and spirit of the Constitution.

But who is to determine whether the advice that is tendered is in such conformity. There is the rub. It can well be urged that as the President on the one hand and the Union Council of Ministers and/or the Union Prime Minister on the other, would be both involved in the matter so the opinion of neither as to the Constitutionality of the advice can be taken to be final and determinative. Article 143 provides that the President may refer to the Supreme Court for its opinion any question of law or fact which is of such a nature and general importance. It is expedient to obtain the opinion of the Supreme Court thereon. But there is also the provision in Clause (2) of Article 74 to the effect that no court shall enquire as to whether the ministers gave any advice to the President and if so what advice was given. Does this provision of Clause (2) of Article 74 bar even the President from referring the question of the Constitutionality of the advice of the union council of minister and or the Union Prime Minister to the Supreme Court for the latter's opinion under Article 143. This matter is somewhat politically explosive and legally complicated. In this connection a reference may be made to what happened in 1977 when the Janata Government felt that the elected Congress Party Governments of those States wherein the Congress party had failed to get any seat or got only one or two seats at the General Election to the Lok Sabha held in that year had no right whatever to continue to rule in those States. As already stated there is no specific provision in the Constitution of India for the dismissal of the elected party Governments of the Constituent States in such an event as aforesaid. Despite this, an advice was tendered to the acting President Shri. B.D. Jatti, by Shri. Morarji Desai, the Janata Prime Minister, to invoke Article 356 of the Constitution and dismiss the concerned Governments. Shri. B.D. Jatti at first hesitated to act according to the advice so tendered. The Janata Party Prime Minister of the Union then publicly declared that if the acting President failed to act upon the advice tendered to him by the Janata Government of the Union, he the Prime Minister of the Union would appeal to the nation against such reluctance of the acting President. In other words the Prime Minister of the Union made it a political contest between the Council of Ministers on the one side and the acting President on the other to be decided in the court of the Indian people. In view of the fact that the acting President is only a stopgap arrangement until a new President is elected he (the acting President) does not have a position of strength. He is fully conscious that he will have to vacate the office of the President and revert to his office of the Vice President within a period which at best cannot be greater than six months. In short he has feet of clay which cannot allow him to stand up firmly in confrontation with the Council of Ministers and the Union Prime Minister. Naturally, Shri. Jatti caved in and dismissed the governments of the concerned Constituent States. But if there had been a duly elected President in office at that time he could well have well rejected the advice and stood his ground. But in that event a serious political crisis would have arisen for the simple reason that the Union Prime Minister would have come into open and direct conflict with the President of India on an issue in respect of which each one of them held very firm and strong opinion especially in view of the provision of the amended Article 74 which ostensibly requires the President to act in accordance with the advice tendered to him by the Council of Ministers, whereas the President would have felt that he was being asked to act in violation of the oath which bound him to preserve, protect and defend the Constitution and the laws. It may be mentioned here that the General Election to the Lok Sabha had been held only a short time before and so the Union Prime Minister and the Union Council of Ministers could lay claim that they had the mandate of the people of India to rule the Union in accordance with their electoral manifesto, and as a corollary thereof insist that their advice in respect of the dismissal of the elected Governments of the concerned Constituent States must be complied with by the President.

It may be imagined that a parallel situation can arise in future as well. Thus it is evident that if it be taken for granted that the amended Article 74 applies with full force even in the case of the action recommended by the council ministers to be taken by the President in the exercise of the power conferred by Article 356 on him, then in the kind of situation visualized above the President would be faced with the dilemma of complying with the recommendation on the one hand and of remaining loyal to the oath which he had taken before assuming his office as President. Could he in that situation refer the Constitutionality of the advice tendered to him to the Supreme Court for its opinion?

The ban imposed by Article 74 (2) applies to a Court of Justice in the matter of enquiring as to whether any advice was given by the Council of Ministers to the President and if given then what that advice was. But when any question of law or fact is referred to the Supreme Court by the

President for the former's opinion can it be said that the Supreme Court in formulating its opinion in respect of the question so referred is acting as a court of justice. The Supreme Court has itself ruled that when deciding whether a court of inquiry is acting as a court of justice it has to be considered as to whether its order conclusively determines the matter under enquiry or it is merely of recommendatory character which the concerned Government may or may not accept. In the case of the opinion tendered by the Supreme Court on the question referred to it under Article 143, it is admitted that the opinion is not legally binding on the Supreme Court itself when that question comes before it for adjudication in a litigation. In other words that opinion is in the nature of what eminent jurists make of it, but does not by itself have the force of law. It may, therefore, be urged that in formulating that opinion the Supreme Court is not acting as a court of justice but only as a body of eminent jurists. If that view be accepted then the ban imposed by clause (2) of Article 74 would not apply and the President would be fully entitled to refer the question of the Constitutional validity of the advice tendered to him by the Union Council of Ministers in respect of the dismissal of the elected Council of Ministers of any Constituent State in the exercise of the powers conferred by Article 356, to the Supreme Court under Article 143 for the latter's opinion. The President could do so in order to strengthen his position vis a vis the union Council of Ministers and the Union Prime Minister in so far as the opinion of the general people in respect of the correctness of the action of the President in disregarding the advice of the former was concerned. But as already stated the legal position in respect of the ban imposed by Article 74 (2) is somewhat complicated. Thus in the ultimate analysis the President shall have to rely upon his own judgment as to whether the public in general would support him in his action of disregarding the advice tendered to him by the Council of

Ministers (which would ultimately be the advice of the Union Prime Minister) to dismiss the elected government. of a Constituent State in the exercise of the powers conferred by Article 356. This implies that the President would disregard that advice only if and when he would be fully convinced that advice was wholly unconstitutional and that if accepted by him would make him commit a flagrant violation of his oath to preserve, protect and defend the Constitution and the law, and that he had no option but to disregard that advice. In such a situation the action of the President in disregarding that advice cannot and should not be considered to be in violation of the Constitution.

In this connection attention is drawn to the fact that Article 356 of the Constitution is not subject to the amended article 74. What even the amended Article 74 provides is simply the inevitability of the existence of a Council of Ministers at the Union level before it can be held that the machinery provided for the running of the Union Government has been fully set up. Further it also provides that this council shall be legally competent to tender advice to the President as the head of the Union Executive and the President in that capacity shall abide by the advice tendered to him by that Council of Ministers. But it does not provide that the President as an integral element of the Union Parliament shall be bound by the advice of the Council of Ministers. Thus Article 111 is not subject to Article 74. In view of the fact that a legislative Bill can be passed by the two houses of Parliament only if and when it is fully supported by the Union Council of Ministers, there cannot arise any occasion for that Council to tender advice to the President to veto the Bill so passed by the two houses of Parliament. So when Article 111 grants power to the President to veto a legislative Bill so passed by the two houses of Parliament, it contemplates that the President shall exercise that power in accordance with his own individual judgment. Of course, ordinarily, the President as an integral element of the Union Parliament would give due weight to what the two Houses of Parliament have done in respect of the concerned Bill, and would give his assent to that Bill unless he strongly feels that Bill is not in the interest of the Nation or violates even indirectly the spirit of the Constitution.

Again the amended Article 74 does not apply in all its rigour to what the President has to do in pursuance of the powers conferred on him by Articles 352 and 356. As argued earlier the President in exercising the powers under those articles, acts not as a mere head of the Union Executive but as the elected representative and Constitutional authority for both the Union and the Constituent States, that is to say for the entire Indian polity, whereas the Union Council of Ministers and the Union Prime Minister act as the Spokesmen of the political party which has for the time being secured a majority in the Lok Sabha. The advice of the Council of Ministers in respect of the invocation of Article 352 or 356 being tinged with partisan interests is not binding on the President who under those articles has to act as the custodian of the interests of the whole nation. If Article 352 had been subject to Article 74, then there would have been no occasion for the fathers of the Constitution to insert Clause (3) in that Article to provide that no proclamation of emergency would be issued by the President unless the decision of the Union Council of Ministers that such a proclamation should be issued has been communicated to the President. It shows that Article 74 does not have any overriding effect in so far as Article 352 is concerned. What is required is that the Council of Ministers must come to a decision that a proclamation of Emergency should be issued and must communicate that decision to the President before the President proceeds to take any action in the matter of the proclamation of Emergency. But he would issue such a proclamation only when and if he is personally satisfied that an emergency has arisen wherein the safety of India is actually endangered by war or insurrection or such danger is imminent. In Article 356 there is no provision parallel to clause (3) of Article 352. Thus it is evident that in the exercise of the power conferred on him by Article 356 the President has to act in accordance with his own judgment. So it can be legitimately urged that Articles 352 and 356 are not subject to Article 74.

Again Article 368 is not subject to article 74. Under that Article a Constitution Amendment Bill has to be placed before the President for his assent. This implies that the President is an integral element of the constituent authority which is competent to amend the Constitution. The procedure prescribed for the amendment of the Constitution is as aforesaid very much distinct from the legislative process whereby ordinary laws are to be enacted by the Union Parliament. The distinctive features are:

(i)   Two third majority of the members present and voting.

(ii)   Absolute majority of the total membership of each House of Parliament.

(iii)   The mandatory provision for each House of Parliament sitting separately to pass the Constitution bill there being no provision for a joint sitting of the two Houses.

(iv)   The absolute necessity of the Constitution Amendment Bill being approved by the legislatures of more than half the Constituent States in case the constitution bill seeks to amend the provisions of the Constitution specified in proviso to Article 368.

Thus the amendment of the Constitution can be

effected by a specially designated Constitutional process which inevitably carries the implication that the amendment of the Constitution is effected not by a body acting as the union legislature but acting in the nature of a Constituent Assembly. In that machinery the President is an integral Constitutional element, and not a mere head of the Union Executive. He can thus withhold his assent to a Constitution bill notwithstanding the use of 'shall' in the relevant clause of that Article in respect of the assent being given by the President. I feel that this import of the Article 368 must be taken to harmonise it with Article 60 of the Constitution. To say this does not imply that the President shall refuse to give assent to a Constitution Bill which has emerged after going through the prescribed Constitutional process and has been presented to him for his assent simply because he has differences with the Union Council of Ministers and the Union Prime Minister on the necessity of bringing about the proposed amendment or on other political questions. He can withhold his assent only if and when he is firmly convinced that the proposed amendment shall have the inevitable consequence of upturning the basic character of the Constitution itself. Ordinarily such an amendment of the Constitution shall hardly cross successfully the prescribed Constitutional process even if the Union Council of Ministers commands a majority in both the Houses of Parliament for getting the proposed Constitution amendment passed by the two Houses of Parliament. This would be so because the majority of the Constituent States may not be ready to bring about such a radical chance in the Constitution. Consequently the question of the President vetoing a Constitution amendment would arise only in the rare situation in which the Union Council of Ministers succeeds in obtaining the approval of the legislatures of more than half the number of the Constituent States and those assenting States contain only a small minority of the total population of the Indian Union. Such a situation could arise only when and if the election to the Lok Sabha had been held at a time when the political party succeeding in securing a two third majority of seats in the Lok Sabha had secured preponderant support in the States which contain a preponderant majority of the population of the Indian Union at that election, but has lost its popularity in those States by the time the Constitution Amendment bill is passed by the two Houses of Parliament. As things stand today there are more than half the number of the total number of the Constituent States the population of which constitutes but a small minority of the total population of the Indian Union. Thus the total population of the States of Sikkim, Arunachal Pradesh, Meghalaya, Nagaland, Manipur, Mizoram, Tripura, Himachal Pradesh, Haryana, Punjab and Rajasthan would be even less than one third of the total population of the Indian Union even though these States are more than half the number of the total number of the Constituent States of the Indian Union. The Union Council of Ministers may succeed in getting a Constitution Amendment Bill passed by two third majority of the two houses of Parliament and by the legislatures of the above mentioned States the population of which is less than one third of the total population of the Indian Union and place such a Constitution Amendment Bill practically upturning the Constitution for the assent of the President. In that situation would the President be legally bound to give his assent to such a Constitution Amendment Bill notwithstanding his oath to preserve, protect and defend the Constitution? The President can in such a situation legitimately decide to abide by his oath and refuse to give his assent to such a Constitution Amendment Bill. By doing so he would not be incurring any risk of being impeached because the representatives of the States having a preponderant majority of the total population of the Indian Union would not dare to ignore the hostility shown by the legislatures of such States to that Constitution amendment bill and would not en masse support the council of ministers if it decides to impeach the President for his refusal to give his assent to the Constitution Amendment Bill. It is, no doubt, true that such a situation as imagined above is not likely to arise except on the rarest occasion but such an exceptional occasion must be kept in view when interpreting the provisions of Article 368. In short it can be said that the President as an integral element of the prescribed Constitutional machinery for effecting amendments to the Constitution does have the reserve power of vetoing a Constitution Amendment Bill which shall have the inevitable consequence of wholly upturning the Constitution. In this connection it may be mentioned that the Supreme Court of India in the *Kesavananda Bharati case* had decided by majority that a Constitution Amendment which eliminates the basic features of the Constitution shall be invalid. It may be said that the President should instead of entering the political amphitheater, leave the matter in the abovementioned situation to be decided by the Supreme Court. But a judicial proceeding can be commenced only by a party which avers that its interests are prejudiced by the coming of the Constitution Amendment into force. Further a judicial proceeding is extremely expensive and in any case involves considerable delay. Should a conscientious President allow a state of uncertainty to continue for a considerable time in respect of such a radical Constitution Amendment merely to insulate himself from the possibility of any dangerous political consequences to himself? Such a timidity on the part of a President would be extremely undesirable for it would amount to his total failure to discharge the duties of his office. It would seem that no occasion for such passivity on the part of the President need arise if it is Constitutionally recognized by all concerned that the President does possess certain reserve powers to be exercised by him in exceptional circumstances. To give an instance of such an exceptional circumstance the move of Smt. Indira Gandhi to impose

Emergency in 1975 may be mentioned. Smt. Indira Gandhi had been disqualified by the Allahabad High Court from holding the office of the Member of the Lok Sabha. The Allahabad High Court had, no doubt, stayed the operation of its judgment to give time to Smt. Indira Gandhi to appeal to the Supreme Court. The vacation judge of the Supreme Court had passed an order in the appeal filed by Smt. Indira Gandhi that while the judgment of the Allahabad High Court shall stand stayed until such time as the appeal was heard and decided by the Supreme Court, Smt. Indira Gandhi shall not take part in any voting in the Lok Sabha. Thus normally she was to abstain from initiating any radical Constitutional or legal measures which were calculated to benefit herself in so far as the question of the validity of her election to the Lok Sabha was concerned. She could continue as the Union Prime Minister only because of the provision of the Constitution that if a person not a member of either House of Parliament is appointed a minister then he or she must get himself or herself elected as a member of either House of Parliament. Keeping the provisions of Article 75 of the Constitution in view it may be doubted whether this provision of the Constitution was strictly applicable to the case of the Prime Minister. But it cannot be denied that a person who is deprived of the right of vote in the Lok Sabha has no competence to initiate such a radical measure as the imposition of Emergency resulting in the wholesale arrest of the members of the political parties in opposition and the suspension of fundamental rights nor any competence to get radical Constitutional amendments initiated. But Smt. Indira Gandhi personally went to the President at an unusual hour at night with a proclamation imposing Emergency under Article 352 to be signed by the President. That proclamation had not been considered and cleared by the Council of Ministers; but even if it had been cleared by that body, could it be legitimately urged that the President was Constitutionally bound to sign that proclamation without spending any time to satisfy himself that a situation had actually arisen or was indeed imminent in which the safety and security of India was in danger. There had not been any violent insurrection in the country nor was there an imminent danger of such insurrection or even of the breakdown of law and order. It may be added that at that time there was no specific provision in Article 74 that the President shall act in accordance with the advice tendered to him. Could he not have raised the question as to how far a person who stood barred from voting in the Lok Sabha by the order of the Supreme Court had any legitimate claim to ask the President to take such a drastic step which involved the abrogation of the liberty of thousands of persons who had dedicated themselves to the service of the Nation or in any case were responsible citizens. But under the belief that the advice of the Prime Minister, who was the principal spokesman of the Union Council of Ministers, was binding on the President that proclamation was signed by the then President Shri. Fakhruddin Ali Ahmed. Is there any reason to believe that such a situation cannot arise in future and that a person who has been disqualified to be a member of either House of Parliament for a number of years continues to stick to hold the post of Union Prime Minister not only asks the President to impose Emergency under Article 352 but also initiates a process of extensive and radical Constitutional amendment in the emasculated Houses of Parliament and gets the same approved by the members of both the Houses functioning under the fear generated by the suspension of fundamental rights and also gets the same approved by the legislatures of such Constituent States which though number more than half the total number of Constituent States have yet only a small minority of the total population of the Indian Union. The answer to this question could not but be in the negative. Keeping in view the type of political leadership in our country it can be safely anticipated that a situation parallel to what arose in 1975 on the above mentioned disqualification of Smt. India Gandhi is quite likely to arise. The only safeguard for the preservation of the liberties of the people will then be the action of the President to disregard whatever recommendation may have been made by the Council of Ministers led by a disqualified Union Prime Minster for the imposing of Emergency, or for the dismissal of those Governments of the Constituent States wherein political parties opposed to the disqualified Union Prime Minister are running the Government and veto whatever material Constitutional amendments have been rushed through the two Houses of Parliament and got approved by the legislatures of such Constituent States, which though equal more than half of the total number of the Constituent States but have only a small minority of the total population of the Indian Union.

It can therefore legitimately be affirmed in the light of the political developments which have taken place during the last forty years that unless it is recognised by all concerned that the President of India is the ballast of the Constitution and that he possess reserve powers for the preservation, protection, and defence of the Constitution in situations in which it is lashed by political storms and passions there can be no stopping the downward movement of the political and Constitutional machinery of our country. What these reserve powers are have been set out above but may be briefly set out again. These are:-

(a) The President can act in the exercise of his individual judgment in the matter of the appointment of the judges of the Supreme Court and the High courts after getting the advice of the Chief Justice of India and such other Supreme Court Judges as he considers should be consulted in the matter. He may disregard the advice of the Council of Ministers in respect of such appointments, if he feels that the advice tendered by the Union Council of Ministers or the Union Prime Minister is tinged with political bias. No institution or body set up, or possibly envisaged, by the Union Council of Ministers to help the President in making such appointments shall be of much use simply because its composition could be so determined by the Union Council of Ministers or by the Union Prime Minister so as to make it susceptible to political and partisan considerations in the selection of judges for the High Courts and the Supreme Court.

The view expressed also finds support from the observation of the Supreme Court case AIR 1991 SC 631. In a recent case the Supreme Court has also felt that the Chief Justice of India should have primacy in the matter of the appointment of the judges of the Supreme Court and the High Court. The court states that – "In India, however, the judicial institutions, by tradition, have an avowed apolitical commitment and the assurance of non-political complexion of the judiciary cannot be divorced from the process of appointment. Constitutional phraseology of "consultation" has to be understood and expounded consistent with and to promote this Constitutional spirit. The implications are, indeed, vital. The Constitutional values cannot be whittled down by calling the appointment of judges as an executive act. The appointment is rather is the result of collective, Constitutional process. It is a participatory Constitutional function. It is, perhaps, inappropriate to refer to any 'power' or 'right' to appoint judges It is essentially a discharge of a Constitutional trust of which certain Constitutional functionaries are collective repositories. The executive, on whose advice the President acts, as a participant in the process has its own important and effective role. To say that the power to appoint solely vests with the executive and the executive, after bestowing such consideration on the result of consultations with the judicial organ of the state, would be at liberty to take such decision as it may think fit in the matter of appointments is an over simplification of a sensitive and subtle

Constitutional sentience and, if allowed foul play, would be subversive of the doctrine of judicial independence." (AIR 1991 SC 645 known as Subhash Sharma Vs Union of India.)

(b) The President may veto any Bill, which has been passed by both the houses of Parliament if he is clearly of the view that the Bill is prejudicial to the national interest or is likely to bring about the attrition of the Constitution.

(c) The President has to satisfy himself that the recommendation of the Union Council of Ministers for the imposition of emergency or for the dismissal of the elected government of a Constituent State is not made to promote partisan interests of the political party in power at the Union level and that the situation does exist in which resort to Article 352 or Article 356 can be legitimately made. If he has no data for such satisfaction he can reject the recommendation made by the Union Council of Ministers.

(d) The President may dissolve the Lok Sabha if he is satisfied on impeccable evidence that the majority of its members are indulging in corruption or unconstitutional practices. He may do so in the exercise of his individual judgment and in disregard of the wishes of the Union Council of Ministers. He may also exercise his individual judgment to accept or reject the advice of the union Council of Ministers tendered for the dissolution of Lok Sabha in the event of the Union Council of Ministers has lost the confidence of the Lok Sabha, but only when the General Election to the Lok Sabha had taken place a short time before. Ordinarily the Union Council of Ministers led by the Union Prime Minister should have the right to appeal to the people (electorate) against the expression of no - confidence in the union Council of Ministers by the Lok Sabha, and the President should respect that right of the Prime Minister. It may be mentioned that the Prime Minister should have this right of asking for the dissolution of the Lok Sabha in order to be able to exercise sufficient control over the members of his political party to keep them away from any idea or plan of serving personal aggrandisement by threatening to desert the party if their demands for personal advancement or monetary gain are not fulfilled. But at the same time, the President should have the power to decide as to whether the demand for the dissolution of the Lok Sabha is made by the union Prime Minister in circumstances in which an appeal to the Nation against the action of the Lok Sabha in withdrawing its confidence in the Union Prime Minister is justified. Such justification would be obvious if considerable time has elapsed after the General Election to the Lok Sabha and the Union Prime Minister has lost the confidence of the Lok Sabha as a consequence of unscrupulous action of a section of the party to which the Union Prime Minister belongs. In other words the President would normally accede to the demand made by the Union Prime Minister for the dissolution of the Lok Sabha when quite an appreciable portion of its term has already expired and also when it is obvious that the public opinion does not back the action of the majority in the Lok Sabha passing the resolution of no-confidence against the Union Council of Ministers. It is only when it is obvious that the Union Prime Minister makes the demand for the dissolution of the Lok Sabha in circumstances in which it is clear that an appeal to the nation is not justified and an alternative stable ministry can be formed which commands a sizable support in the country and has the backing of a principled majority in the Lok Sabha, that the President may reject the demand made by the defeated Union Prime Minister for the dissolution of the Lok Sabha. In a way this also is a kind of reserve power which may be exercised by the President in exceptional situations.

The President may on his own initiative require the

Union Prime Minister to furnish him information in respect of the decisions taken by the Council of Ministers relating to administrative problems and legislative proposals. The President may also require the Union Prime Minister to place any question for the consideration of the Council of Ministers on which a minister has already taken a decision but which had not been considered by the Council of Ministers.

(e) Under Article 86(2) the President may on his initiative send a message to a House of Parliament in respect of a Bill then under consideration in any House of the Parliament and the House to which message has been sent shall be bound to consider the matter which the message required it to consider.

(f) The President may also exercise his individual judgment in giving his assent to any Bill passed by the legislature of a state but reserved under Article 201 for the consideration of the President. The object of such reservation is to ensure that no state legislature may enact a law, which prejudicially affects the national interest. Naturally, the Union Council of Ministers shall be scrutinizing such a reserved Bill and decide whether it does or does not endanger national interest, and tender its advice to the President accordingly. Ordinarily the President must give considerable weight to the advice so tendered. But as there is every probability that the political and economic approach of the state Government and that of the Union Government are likely to differ to a considerable extent, so there is also a probability that the opinion of the Union Government, as formulated by the Council of Ministers may be influenced by that difference of approach only so the President as the custodian of the interests of both the Constituent States and the Union shall have to keep that factor in view, when deciding to accept or reject the advice tendered by the Union Council of Ministers. It may be emphasized again that the matter being extremely delicate in nature, the President shall have to act with utmost caution and after deep consideration of all the factors involved in assenting or vetoing the State Bill reserved by the Governor of the concerned state for his consideration. It would be, however, on the rarest of rare occasions when the President shall have the occasion to disregard the advice of the Union Council of Ministers in regard to this matter. What is urged here is only that the President does have the power to exercise his individual judgment in the matter though on rarest of rare occasions. It would be evident from what has been urged above that the powers of the President are in the nature of reserve power which come into operation only when and if he is faced with a situation in which he shall be violating his oath if he were to act in accordance with the advice tendered to him by the Union Council of Ministers. This makes his role as the ballast of the ship of state which keeps it on even keel without in any way hampering the working of the Master of the ship of the state. If this fact is recognized by all concerned, then there would be hardly any occasion for any confrontation occurring between the President on the one side and the Union Council of Ministers on the other, and would at the same time prevent any action by the Union Council of Ministers and the Union Prime Minister which directly or indirectly leads to the attrition of the institutions set up by the Constitution of India.

Prof. Balkrishna receiving an award from President Dr. Rajendra Prasad.

ABOUT THE AUTHOR

Prof. Balkrishna - 8 September 1907 to 1 May 1993.

Prof. Balkrishna was a lecturer in History and Political Science at Meerut College, Meerut; and later Professor and Head of Department - Political Science and History at Birla College, Pilani. His education qualifications included M.A. in History and Political Science; and L.L.B.

At Birla College, Pilani, Prof Balkrishna came into contact with Dr. Rajendra Prasad who was there writing his book India Divided and had the opportunity of assisting him in the task. The book mentions Prof Balkrishna's name in the Preface.

Impressed by Prof Balkrishna's work, Dr. Rajendra Prasad invited him to Delhi where he joined the Secretariat of the Constituent Assembly of India and was entrusted the work of preparing the Constitution (which was being enacted in English) in Hindi. He was made Member Secretary for a Committee of which Dr. Ghanshyam Singh Gupta was chairman. Other members were Rahul Sankrityayan, Dr. Suniti Kumar Chatterji and Dr. Raghuni. He had to work very hard to keep pace with the progress of the English version. He was handicapped because there was hardly any staff to assist him. Still he was able to get the Hindi version printed in time.

After the Secretariat was wound up, he joined the personal staff of the President of India as Press Attaché, and later on functioned as his Deputy Secretary. Prof Balkrishna assisted the President in preparation of his public speeches and also attended the legal work entrusted by the President. He was sent to Ministry of Law to initiate the preparation of the authoritative texts of Central Laws.

As a follow up of Presidential Order of 27th April 1960 to Government of India constituted two Standing Committees.

1. The Commission for Scientific and Technical

Terminology and

2. The official Language (Legislative) commission. Prof Balkrishna was its first Member Secretary and continued to be so till 1972 and twice after some intervals.

As Member Secretary of OLL WC, he laid down the foundation of Pan Indian vocabulary for use in all Indian languages, as far as possible. During his tenure Central Acts were translated in Hindi and many other languages.

He drew up a scheme for publications of text books for LLB classes and for publication of judgement of the Supreme Court and the High Courts in Hindi. He was the first editor of the these journals containing reports of judgements. In the initial days when Sub Editor, Assistant Editors, Proof Readers had yet to be recruited he worked for almost 12-14 hours a day for months together and translated the material, read the proof and arranged for printing.

He had a very analytical mind, sharp memory, ability to grasp quickly and an untiring capacity to work without any regard to his health.

It was during his tenure that authoritative texts in Hindi of important acts, e.g., The Indian Penal Code, The Criminal Procedure Code, Transfer of Property Act, The evidence Act etc. were published.

Prof Balkrishna has contributed articles on political and Constitutional questions. After retirement he wrote a book in Hindi on Jurisprudence, which published posthumously. The Ministry of Law awarded a prize for the work.

He was a Life member of Nagari Pracharini Sabha, Kashi, Institute for Constitutional and Parliamentary Studies, Asiatic Society of Bombay; and a Member of Indian law Institute, Delhi.

Get Published with Frontier India

Do you want to get your book or thesis published? You might even want to republish your book which is currently out of print.. Frontier India Technology as a publisher, distributor and retailer of books, offers a complete range of publishing, editorial, and marketing services that helps you as an author to take his or her book to the reader.

Getting your work published is a wish for many for reasons including profit earning, self-satisfaction, popularity and other good reasons. We will offer you choices based on your needs. Get in touch with us at frontierindia@gmail.com.

Our Recently Published Books include :

An Indian Air force Recollects by Wing Co P.K. Karayi (Retd.) ISBN: 978-8193005507

Warring Navies – India and Pakistan (International Edition) – by Cmde Ranjit B. Rai (Retd.). Joseph P. Chacko. ISBN: 978-8193005545

Basics of marriage Management by Walter E Vieira. ISBN: 978-8193005514

Beat That Exam Fever – Succeed in Examinations by Walter E Vieira. ISBN: 978-8193005538

Ordinary Stocks, Extra Ordinary Profits by Anand S. ISBN: 978-8193005521

Foxtrot to Arihant – The Story of Indian Navy's Submarine Arm by Joseph P. Chacko. ISBN: 978-8193005552

Foxtrots of the Indian Navy by Cmde P.R Franklin. ISBN: 978-8193005576

A Nation and its Navy at War by Cmde Ranjit Rai. ISBN: 978-8193005583

www.ingramcontent.com/pod-product-compliance
Lightning Source LLC
Chambersburg PA
CBHW031358160726
47993CB00003B/1011